Cambridge IGCSE®
Physics

Practical Teacher's Guide

Gillian Nightingale

CAMBRIDGE
UNIVERSITY PRESS

CAMBRIDGE
UNIVERSITY PRESS

University Printing House, Cambridge CB2 8BS, United Kingdom

Cambridge University Press is part of the University of Cambridge.

It furthers the University's mission by disseminating knowledge in the pursuit of education, learning and research at the highest international levels of excellence.

Information on this title: education.cambridge.org

© Cambridge University Press 2017

First published 2017

20 19 18 17 16 15 14 13 12 11 10 9 8 7 6 5 4 3

Printed in Great Britain by CPI Group (UK) Ltd, Croydon CR0 4YY

A catalogue record for this publication is available from the British Library

ISBN 978-1-316-61108-1 Paperback

The questions, answers and annotation in this title were written by the author and have not been produced by Cambridge International Examinations.

In an examination, the marks granted might differ from the ones given to the answers found in this material.

....

....

Contents

Introduction

Physics is an interactive and exciting subject that lends itself to practical investigations and activities in the laboratory. However, teachers can often lack confidence in leading practical investigations for a variety of reasons, such as time constraints, lack of resources, reliability of the experiments being performed and a lack of practical knowledge. For students wishing to advance in physics beyond Cambridge IGCSE, they need to have the skills, experience and confidence in designing and conducting investigations. Whilst this can be taught through textbooks and other forms of media, a more hands-on approach will encourage student engagement and passion for the subject.

The aim of this book is to give you, the teacher, confidence to attempt a wide variety of practical work with your students. Many of the investigations are relatively simple and require little specialist equipment alternatives are also suggested where possible. It is understood that, even with the best of intentions, it will not always be possible to complete every investigation in this book successfully. Limitations of both equipment and time often place pressure on your ability to deliver practical work. To enable students to develop skills, even if they are actually unable to complete the practical work, the CD-ROM provides sample data that can be used with and by students. The data on the CD-ROM can be used when either the practical cannot be completed or the experiment goes awry and does not provide useful data.

This Teacher's Guide has been written for Cambridge IGCSE physics teachers and technicians, to support the Practical Workbook. The Practical Workbook caters for both the practical paper and the alternative to the practical paper. The chapters mirror the Cambridge University Press Cambridge IGCSE coursebook and the skills required for each practical support the syllabus. The early chapters of the book include a large amount of scaffolding to support students as they first begin practical work. This is gradually reduced through the remainder of the book. Each skill area is revisited in different contexts, to ensure that students have plenty of opportunities to develop each one.

Students learn most by doing and being active so, although demonstrations are suggested at times to allow for the differences in student ability, letting the students complete the investigations for themselves is strongly encouraged.

Where practical investigations and or/related answers in this Teacher's Guide contain extended syllabus material, this has been identified by a thin vertical bar in the margin next to the relevant material.

Gradient calculations in all topics are extension material and are used in the Practical Workbook to allow students to gain confidence in their graphical skills, and to become comfortable with visualising relationships between variables.

Each investigation has a section comprising questions to get students to think about what their results mean and how they can improve upon the methods that they have used. Encouraging the students to work like physicists will greatly improve their ability to think like physicists.

The Safety section at the start of this book outlines some basic safety precautions; specific safety issues are highlighted for each investigation. The inclusion of these notes does not remove from the teacher the responsibility for ensuring that all work attempted by the students is safe. A degree of judgment will be required in respect of each student's ability to follow instructions and work safely.

Safety section

Despite the fact that Bunsen burners and chemicals are used on a regular basis, the science laboratory is one of the safest classrooms in a school. This is due to the emphasis on safety and the adherence to precautions and procedures resulting from regular risk assessment.

Responsibility for all safety matters rests with the teacher and their technicians. The safety precautions set out in this guide are simply guidance towards your own full risk assessment that you must carry out and record.

Different educational authorities set different standards and guidelines. It is important that the minimum safety standards are met as set out by your local education authority or educational provider before conducting any practical investigation. Use the following sources for further guidance as part of your laboratory risk assessment procedures.

- **Consortium of Local Education Authorities for the Provision of Science Services (CLEAPSS)** provides support in practical science.
- Control of Substances Hazardous to Health (**COSHH**) offers further guidance relative to UK law and regulations. This is an excellent guide, if you wish to carry out a thorough risk assessment for your laboratory or department.
- **Material Safety Data Sheets (MSDS)** provide detailed information about the different substances and materials that you may use. They include information such as safe storage, hazard rating, expiration times, fire hazards, preventative action, emergency action – and much more about any substance. These should be provided by your technician, with the materials or solutions every time they are delivered to your classroom.
- **Hazards** also offer the important safety, storage, and emergency action information for chemicals used in the science laboratory.

The safety information provided in the student workbook comprises basic precautions to be followed in the laboratory. The information is also designed to help students develop the necessary planning skills to help to prepare for examination in this area. The safety precautions provided in this teacher resource are intended to guide you in delivering safe science investigations in your laboratory.

It is worthwhile emphasising safety during demonstrations and also making students aware of the consequences of not following the safety advice. Take time to explain to students what action to take in the event of spills or breakages, as well as how to dispose of chemical waste safely.

The new hazard codes will be used where relevant and in accordance with information provided by CLEAPSS.

C	=	corrosive	**MH**	=	moderate hazard
HH	=	health hazard	**T**	=	acutely toxic
F	=	flammable	**O**	=	oxidising
N	=	hazardous to the aquatic environment			

1 Making measurements

Throughout this chapter students will be expected to:
● take accurate readings from a range of measuring devices
● take a sufficient range of measurements, repeating where necessary, to obtain an average (mean) value
● present and analyse data graphically.

Practical investigation 1.1 Estimating measurements

Planning the investigation

In this investigation, students will:
● use and describe the use of rules and measuring cylinders to find a length or a volume
● use and describe the use of clocks and devices, both analogue and digital, for measuring an interval of time

This practical can be taught in conjunction with the theory.
Duration: 15–20 minutes

Setting up for the investigation

Student grouping: 2–4 students per group, depending on class size.

Each group will need: metre rule, stopwatch, a micrometer screw gauge, thermometer, top-pan balance, newton scale, micrometer screw gauge, 30 cm rule
Review how to use a micrometer screw gauge at the beginning of the practical.
Students will require additional support using the micrometer screw gauge

Measuring equipment should be distributed around the classroom to avoid congestion.
Remind students that dropping the balls will distort them.

Safety considerations
● Ensure students keep the floor clear, for example, free from bags, to reduce the risk of tripping.
● Keep the classroom door closed when students measuring its width to prevent fingers being trapped in the hinges.
● Complete a dynamic safety assessment to ensure no risk to students.

Key discussion points for this investigation
● **Precision:** Why use a micrometer screw gauge, rather than a ruler, to measure the diameter of a wire? Why might it be important for an electrician to be more precise with the thickness of cable measurements than an lift engineer, for example?
● **Accuracy**: Why are accurate measurements important? How might an inaccurate measurement affect the outcome of a 100 m race, the value of a diamond, the weight of a gold bar?
● **How can students improve accuracy?** When measuring with a ruler, students should ensure that the ruler is parallel to the object they are measuring, and that their eyes are level with the measurement they are taking, to reduce the effect of a parallax error. When timing events with a short time span, they should record the time for ten events and divide by ten, to find the average time for one.

- **Methods of measurement**: Students should consider alternatives. How many ways could they find the volume of a cube? Which method is more accurate? Why might they choose displacement over length measurement and calculation?

Common errors when conducting this investigation

Set each group a different task, to help avoid congestion around the classroom. They will need to observe the progress of each group to ensure there is no clustering at the more popular tasks.

Supporting your students

Discuss how to use the micrometer screw gauge. Reading the scale might be an issue for some students. Set up the micrometer and invite students to read the scale, to ensure that they understand how to do it. If a student is really struggling, provide digital calipers for them to use as an interim measure.

Challenging your students

In the field of medicine, accurate measurement by doctors helps to ensure that patients are diagnosed correctly and treated effectively. Investigate ways in which doctors use technology to make accurate measurements and how inaccurate measurements can affect patient care. Prepare a two-minute presentation for the class.

Each year billions of goods are sold, based on a measurement of quantity. Why is it important that all traders use accurate equipment to measure their products? How might a business be affected if its measurement system was incorrect by just one per cent? Investigate the impact on the revenue for a business if its fuel pump's measurement system was incorrect by one per cent, based on the pump providing 100 cars with 30 litres of fuel every week for one year.

Answers to workbook questions

1   Students record their results in the table.
2   Students comment on their estimated and measured results. They make reference to the limits of accuracy of the measuring equipment.
3   Students calculate the volume of the glass block, based on their measurements using the micrometer screw gauge.
4   Students calculate the volume of the glass block, based on their measurements using rulers.
5   A micrometer screw gauge gives a more precise result than a ruler. This increased degree of accuracy is then carried into the calculation.
6   Students suggest alternative methods of measurement.
7   Micrometer screw gauge precision is correct to 0.01 cm or 0.1 mm; 30 cm ruler precision is correct to 1 mm; metre ruler precision is correct to 1 mm; stopwatch precision is correct to 0.01 s (depending on stopwatch used).

Practical investigation 1.2
Determining π

Planning the investigation

In this investigation students will:
- obtain an average value for a small distance and for a short interval of time (including the period of a pendulum) by measuring multiples
- present data graphically, drawing a line of best fit and calculating a gradient.

This can be taught after basic theory.

Duration: 45–50 minutes, including graph drawing and analysis

Setting up for the investigation

Student grouping: 2–3 depending on class size

Each group will need: 6 modelling clay balls of varying sizes, micrometer screw gauge, string, ruler

The balls of modelling clay should range in size, from a marble up to the maximum size that will fit within the micrometer screw gauge.

Equipment should be laid out on either side of the room. Modelling clay balls should be kept in a box to provide a place where students can collect a ball, returning it when they have used it and collecting the next one.

In this investigation, the students are asked to measure and calculate the diameters and circumferences of six modelling clay balls. Students measure the diameter at three points across the ball and then find an average (mean) value. They use string to measure the circumference of the ball. They then plot a graph of diameter against circumference, draw a line of best fit and calculate its gradient. This should give the value of π (approximately 3.14).

They will need to take measurements of the balls before the lesson so that they have a set of results from which to work.

Safety considerations

- Remind students not to throw the modelling clay balls, to prevent injury to other students.
- Advise students how to use a micrometer screw gauge correctly, to prevent injury to themselves and other students.

Suggested discussion points for this practical

- **Rationale for multiple measurements of diameter across the ball:** For example, to ensure an average diameter of each ball, as the diameter may not be uniform, or to reduce errors in measurement for the smaller balls.
- **Scaling for the plotting of graphs:** Acceptable scales are based on a multiple of 2, 5 or 10 and should allow the plot to take up $\frac{3}{4}$ of the graph grid.
- **Lines of best fit:** Discuss how to draw one, why they are used, use of a pencil and ruler, and so on.
- **Gradient calculation:** Remind the students how to calculate a gradient, the relevance of the gradient in this practical (represents π).
- **Directly proportional:** What does this mean? How would this be represented on a graph?

Supporting your students

Students often struggle to read micrometer screw gauge. Prepare paper printouts showing a micrometer screw gauge and provide examples for the class to read, using the paper versions as a starter for the session. These can then also be used for one-to-one support during the practical.

Scaling of the graph and calculation of the gradient might present problems. Starter exercises could focus on a 'What scale would you choose?' activity, where example results are given and students have to choose the appropriate scale. They could also be given sample gradient calculations.

Challenging your students

Students can be introduced to the general equation $y = mx + c$ as a means of checking their results. Investigate how racing-car team engineers use this relationship to increase the performance of their cars. Produce an A4 leaflet explaining the principle and how it is applied in Formula 1.

1   Students record their results in the table.
2   Students plot their graphs.
3   Students draw a line of best fit.
4   Straight-line graph through the origin.
5   Yes. This is because the line of best fit is a straight line through the origin.
6   Students calculate
    $$\frac{\text{change in circumference values}}{\text{change in diameter values}}$$
    or use the triangle method, the gradient should be approximtely 3.14.
7   Yes, because the gradient of the graph is equal to π.
8   Mark a line on the ball, start to roll the ball in a line along a ruler and measure one complete rotation.
9   The marking the ball method. String might not be tight round the ball, or might not lie exactly around the widest part, so might give an incorrect measurement of diameter.
10 The balls might not be uniformly spherical.
11 Errors in measurement might affect the result.

Practical investigation 1.3
The simple pendulum

Planning the investigation

In this investigation students will:
● obtain an average value for a small distance and for a short interval of time (including the period of a pendulum) by measuring multiples.

This can be taught after theory.

Duration: 20 minutes

Setting up for the investigation

Each group will need: pendulum bob, string, 2 small rectangular pieces of wood or corkboard, clamp stand, clamp, boss, stopwatch, ruler

During the experiment, students should fix the string of the pendulum between the jaws of the clamp.

Use a secondary C-clamp to fix the clamp stand to the bench for safety to prevent toppling.

This investigation considers the relationship between the length of a pendulum and its time period of oscillation. Students are asked to vary the length of the pendulum string and record the time period of oscillation each time. Students will be expected to measure the time taken for ten swings. They will repeat this three times for each length and take an average. Dividing this average by ten will give the time taken for one oscillation.

Safety considerations

● Show students the correct way to swing the pendulum. Demonstrate pulling the pendulum so the string makes a small angle from the vertical and releasing gently, to prevent students releasing the pendulum aggressively. If you have a particularly lively class, suggest goggles should be worn for the practical investigation.
● Fix the clamp stand to the desk or bench with the C-shaped clamp, to prevent it toppling and causing injury.

Key discussion points for this investigation

● **How to measure the time period of one oscillation when the practical equipment is set up:** Discuss why multiple measurements will reduce error in reading.

- **How accuracy in measurements can be improved**: For example, by counting as the bob passes a fixed point or fiducial marker, or passes through its lowest point.
- **The variable that affects the time period**: Graphical representation of these relationships (time period and length) can be presented to the students to discuss the idea of direct proportion when considering $\frac{T^2}{l}$ or what a curve represents if T^2 is plotted against l.

Common errors when conducting the investigation

The pendulum should be released through small amplitudes. If it is released through a large amplitude the swing will not be periodic and will give incorrect readings, which will affect the results. Discuss this with students before starting the investigation.

Students might struggle to remain focused when recording the number of oscillations. A prior discussion about fiducial markers is recommended. Students might count the beginning of the oscillation as 'one', when they need to wait for a complete oscillation, with the pendulum returning to its initial position, before counting. This might cause their results to be smaller than the actual time period.

Supporting your students

Some students might struggle to understand why counting more oscillations reduces error in the final measurements. Use analogies to help the students understand that the error due to human reaction time will remain constant. However, if they count more oscillations, that percentage error will represent a smaller proportion of time than when just recording one oscillation.

Challenging your students

Ask students to investigate the effect of changing the mass of the bob rather than the length of the string. Ask them to consider the potential variables they will need to keep the same.

Students should create a short presentation of their results for the class.

Foucault's pendulum is probably the most famous pendulum in science. Investigate the significance of Foucault's pendulum and the impact it has had on our knowledge of the Earth.

Answers to workbook questions

1. Students record their results in the table.
2. Students sketch their graphs, with length on the horizontal axis and time period on the vertical axis, to produce a roughly horizontal line.
3. Results should show that mass has a negligible effect on the time period of the pendulum.
4. Students may suggest that the length of the string and the angle from which it is released affect the time period.
5. Add in a fiducial marker and count as it passes this point.
6. It reduces the significance of any errors in measurement on time if the number of oscillations recorded increases.

Practical investigation 1.4
Calculating the density of liquids

Planning the investigation

In this investigation students will:
- recall and use the equation $\rho = \frac{m}{V}$
- describe an experiment to determine the density of a liquid and of a regular 3d solid and make the necessary calculations
- predict whether an object will float, based on density data.

This practical can be conducted in conjunction with teaching the theory.

Duration: 45–60 minutes including graphical analysis

Setting up for the investigation

Grouping: 2–4 depending on class size

Each group will need: 100 ml measuring cylinder, oil, salt-water solution, water, balance

250 ml measuring cylinders can be used, in place of the 100 ml ones.

Any oil that is readily available such as baby oil, cooking oil, rapeseed oil may be used.

Any salt-water solution will have a different density to water, heavily salted water could be used containing food colouring to distinguish it from unsalted water, allow 100 ml per pair.

Equipment should be set out around the classroom, evenly distributed so it is easily accessible and prevents crowding. Dispense the oil and salt-water solution into labelled beakers to prevent students needing to queue for the bottle.

In this investigation the students are asked to record the mass of a fluid for increasing volumes. They will do this for oil, water and a salt-water solution. Students will then be expected to plot their results as a graph of mass against volume. The gradients of the graphs represent the densities of the fluids. From this, students will be asked to determine which solution will float on top of which.

Safety considerations

HH

- Students should wear goggles to ensure no oil or salt-water solution gets into eyes. Rinse immediately if this occurs.

- Clear any spillages immediately to prevent slipping.
- Ask your students if any of them have allergies to rapeseed oil and warn them how important it is that the oil doesn't touch their mouths.

Suggested discussion points for this investigation

- **Taking readings from the bottom of meniscus**: Explain what the meniscus is.
- **Graph skills**: Discuss choosing a scale, drawing the line of best fit, calculating gradient.
- **Discussion**: If students had the same volume of each of the fluids, how could they determine the densities? Why is it important to measure equal volumes?
- **Discussion**: How might temperature affect density? Why would an increase in temperature cause a decrease in density? How is this related to convection?

Common errors when conducting the investigation

Advise students to measure the mass of the water first, then the salt-water solution. then the oil. This is primarily because the water is the easiest to remove from the cylinder, so there will be no residue to affect the mass measurement.

The balance should be tared (zeroised) at the beginning of the experiment to take account of the mass of the measuring cylinder. It should be done again when students start with the next fluid. Students often forget to tare, or continually zero throughout the experiment, which will give them incorrect results.

Students should plot all three graphs on the one grid and should label each line of best fit as they go along so they are clear which line is which.

Supporting your students

Students will generally struggle with drawing lines of best fit and calculating gradients. Discuss how to calculate a gradient at the beginning of the session and leave a worked example on the board throughout, as a point of reference.

One-to-one help might be required when discussing lines of best fit. It is beneficial to have worksheets with sample plots for students to practise drawing lines of best fit, as an aid.

Challenging your students

Give students some additional items, such as a small piece of crayon, a piece of dried pasta, a paperclip and a small piece of wood. Students should layer the fluids they have used, based on their densities, and place the objects in the mix. The objects should settle in different layers. Students should explain, in terms of density, why this has happened and what this implies about the density of the items in comparison to the fluids in which they are suspended.

Students can use the internet or books to research the Galilean thermometer. They can then design a practical that investigates the effect of temperature on the density of fluids.

Answers to exam-style questions

1. eye level with $8\,cm^3$ line [2]
2. $8\,cm^3$ [1]
3. $\rho = \dfrac{m}{V}, \dfrac{65.01}{8}$ [1], 8.13 [1] g/cm^3 (1)
4. steel [1]

   Total marks [7]

Answers to workbook questions

1. Students record their results in the table.
2. Students sketch their graphs of volume against mass for each of the liquids.
3. Students draw and label the line of best fit on each graph.
4. The graph that has the steepest gradient will have the highest density. The gradient of the salt-water solution is the steepest showing that salt water has the highest density of all the solutions.
5. Water $1\,g/cm^3$, oil $0.92\,g/cm^3$, salt water $1.03\,g/cm^3$
6. Salt-water solution, water, oil
7. Students suggest reasons: errors in measurement, errors in calculations.
8. The student is incorrect. Results from this investigation show that oil is less dense than salt water so would float on the surface of the sea water. This would make it possible to separate the two.

2 Describing motion

This chapter contains investigations on:

◆ **1.2** Motion

Throughout this chapter your students will be expected to:
- manipulate apparatus to obtain measurements
- record observations systematically, for example in a table, using appropriate units and to a consistent and appropriate degree of precision
- present and analyse data graphically, including the use of best-fit lines where appropriate and the determination of a gradient of a line

Practical investigation 2.1 Average speed

Planning the investigation

During this investigation your students will:
- calculate the average speed using the equation
$$\text{speed} = \frac{\text{total distance}}{\text{total time}}$$
- plot and interpret a speed–time graph or a distance–time graph
- recognise from the shape of a distance–time graph the relative speed of the body.

This can be taught in conjunction with theory.

Duration: 45 minutes

Grouping: Groups of 6 (one student every 20 m marker and one runner) unless doing the experiment as a class.

Setting up for the investigation

Each group will need: chalk or cones, measuring tape, stopwatches

Anything that will remain in place as a temporary marker may be used instead of chalk or cones.

The measuring tape is used to measure at least 20 m intervals.

The students will be asked to record the time taken to run 100 m, using stopwatches placed at 20 m intervals (20 m, 40 m, 60 m, 80 m, 100 m). Talk through the investigation with the students beforehand to ensure they understand the method. They will use the data obtained to plot and analyse a distance–time graph.

Safety considerations

Ensure that the students who are sprinting, are appropriately warmed up so that the risk of soft-tissue injury is minimised.

There are no inherent safety considerations but an onsite risk assessment will need to be done for trip hazards.

Common errors when conducting the investigation

For this to generate worthwhile data, all five 'timer' students must start their stopwatches at the same time; students will often struggle to achieve this. Discuss signals that students could use to ensure they all start the stopwatch at the same time, for example, the student at the 100 m marker acts as the starter; all the other students wait for a signal from this student to start their stopwatches, or begin running.

Supporting your students

Students will particularly struggle with the analysis of the graph. Students should be able to calculate the speed of each of the sections by using the equation $v = \frac{d}{t}$, but may need to be reminded that for any particular section the distance travelled is 20 m and they will need to find the time for this 20 m by subtracting the previous time reading from the overall reading.

More able students will recognise that drawing a line point to point will allow them to calculate the gradient and thus the speed for this section.

Some students may struggle with the gradient calculation for the average speed across the 100 m. A worked example can be provided or students can use $v = \dfrac{d}{t}$ for this if they do not want to practice the supplementary material.

Challenging your students

Devise a theoretical laboratory-based practical to measure both average and instantaneous speed. The equipment they would have at their disposal is a pair of light gates, a trolley, pulley, masses, card and sticky tape. Comparing the average speed of Usain Bolt over 100 m and the average speed of a fighter jet over its first 100 m, which would win a 100 m race? Prepare a quick presentation for the class, explaining the findings of their calculations

Key discussion points for this investigation

- **The difference between instantaneous and average speed**: How could students adapt the investigation to calculate the instantaneous speed? They will need to understand the difference between instantaneous speed and average speed and how the method would differ practically. To measure instantaneous speed the students would have to measure, in theory, the distance travelled by the person in a particular instant and how long it took them to so this. Students need to realise that an instant in time is extremely small, so would be extremely difficult to measure. The best example of instantaneous speed measurement is the speedometer in a car.
- **Measuring time accurately**: How will students ensure that all timers start their stopwatches at the same time? How can they adapt the investigation to make it more precise, accurate and reliable?
- **Graph drawing**: The key points for drawing graphs should be reiterated here.
- The investigation records the average speed, hence the straight-line connections. What would the graph look like if the person were changing speed, accelerating or decelerating?
- **Distance–time graphs**: The gradient represents the speed. Constant speed is represented by a straight, positive gradient.

Answers to workbook questions

1 The students record their results in the table.
2 The students use the data from their table to plot a distance–time graph of their results.
3 The section with the steepest gradient represents the section in which the runner was moving fastest, as the gradient represents the speed, or the section with the smallest increase in time represents the section in which the runner was moving fastest as they covered the 20min a smaller amount of time.
4 The triangulation method or change in vertical values or horizontal values should be evident, or, evidence of using $V = \dfrac{d}{t}$ provided. Check students' results.
5 Calculate the distance travelled and the time taken in an instant. This would be difficult to measure.
6 $\dfrac{\text{total distance travelled}}{\text{total time taken}} = \dfrac{100}{\text{student answer}}$
7 Precision is dependent on the instruments used. Precision can be increased by using smaller divisions on the instruments used.
8 Immediately the starter signals the runner to start to move, the timers start their stopwatches.
9 The graph would appear as a curve with an increasing gradient. The curve would get steeper as time went on.

Practical investigation 2.2
Velocity–time graphs using ticker tape

Planning the investigation

During this investigation your students will:

- recognise linear motion for which the acceleration is constant
- calculate the area under a velocity–time graph to work out the distance travelled for motion with constant acceleration
- calculate acceleration from the gradient of a velocity–time graph.

This investigation should be conducted after the theory has been taught.

Duration: 1 hour including drawing graph

Grouping: Three to five students per group

Setting up for the investigation

Each group will need: trolley, ticker timer, ticker tape, power pack, ramp, plain coloured paper, scissors, glue, sticky tape

Trolley wheels need to be able to run freely.

Ticker timer usually ticks at a frequency of 50 Hz, although some work at 100 Hz, in which case, change the information given to students accordingly.

A carbon paper disc will be required unless the ticker timer is self-inking; spots can be faint so check that the spots are visible on all tapes being used before the lesson.

Anything can be used as a ramp, provided it is smooth so the trolley can move freely; books can be used to raise the ramp to an incline if stands are not available. Coloured paper allows for clearer visibility of ticker tape, although white paper can be used.

Equipment should be set up as in Fig. 2.1 beforehand, if possible. Students should spread their groups out around the classroom so that the trolleys will not crash into one another.

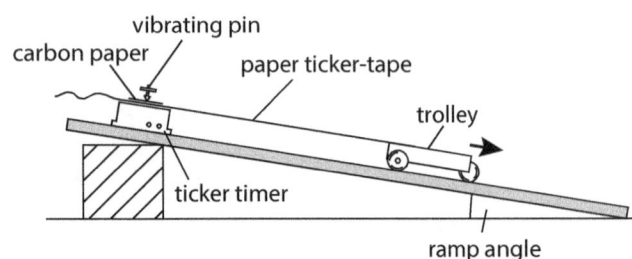

Figure 2.1

Each student will be asked to construct a velocity-time graph. They will use ticker tape from one run of a trolley down an angled ramp. Each 10-dot strip will represent 0.2 seconds, based on a 50 Hz ticker timer. Its length represents the distance travelled. Students will need to stick the strips in order onto a set of velocity–time axes to produce a bar chart.

Safety considerations

The ramps are heavy. If students – rather than the technicians – are setting up, ensure that two students carry the ramps together.

Ensure that a buffer is placed at the end of the ramp to stop the trolley falling and damaging the floor or students' feet.

Common errors when conducting the investigation

Ticker tape dots may be difficult to see, so sometime students miss the odd interval. Ensure students double check counts before cutting.

Cutting on the correct dots: stress that students must cut through the eleventh dot. This then becomes the first dot on the next strip.

Students might forget to label the ticker tape strips as they cut them up, then become confused about the order in which they need to stick them.

At the beginning of the run and at the end, when the trolley slows or hits the buffer, dots are often clustered together. Advise students to start counting from when there is a clear separation between the dots (at 1 mm).

Supporting your students

Students might struggle to visualise the end result of this experiment. An example graph has been constructed and added to the CD-ROM. This gives a good visual guide on how to construct it, how to draw in the line of best fit and how to calculate the gradient.

Challenging your students

Ask students to predict what a velocity–time graph for a trolley going up the ramp would look like. They can then carry out this practical again, using the ticker tape. The ticker timer and tape should be moved to the bottom of the ramp and the trolley should be given a push up the ramp and allowed to run down again freely.

Key discussion points for this investigation

- **Gradient calculation**: What does the gradient on a velocity–time graph represent? Consider a positive gradient, negative gradient, curved line, straight line.
- **Area underneath a velocity–time graph**: Why does it represent the distance travelled? Each strip represents how far the trolley has actually travelled in that section of time. The trolley's increasing velocity is clear to see as the distance increases significantly with each strip. Students can calculate the actual distance by measurement and also by a line through the points. Why might they be different?

Answers to workbook questions

1. Students should cut the ticker tape into 10-dot sections, labelling them in the order in which they are cut from the start of the tape.
2. Refer to the example of a Velocity time graph on CD-ROM for guidance.
3. Refer to the example of a Velocity time graph on CD-ROM for guidance.
4. See students' graphs.
5. Columns are increasing in height, there is a positive gradient so velocity is increasing.
6. See students' graphs.
7. Students calculate the gradients of their graphs; units cm/s^2.
8. Students calculate the area under their graphs; units cm.
9. Started counting the dots from where a pattern was visible, started counting where the gaps were clear, used a fresh carbon paper disc.
10. The ramp is not steep enough so the trolley has moved at a constant velocity. Increase the gradient of the ramp.

Answers to exam-style questions

1. Check suitable scale has been chosen. [1]
   Axes should be labelled, including units. [1]
   Correct plot to $\frac{1}{2}$ square. [2]
   Line of best fit. [1]
2. Neatness of plot and line of best – are they all clear? [1]

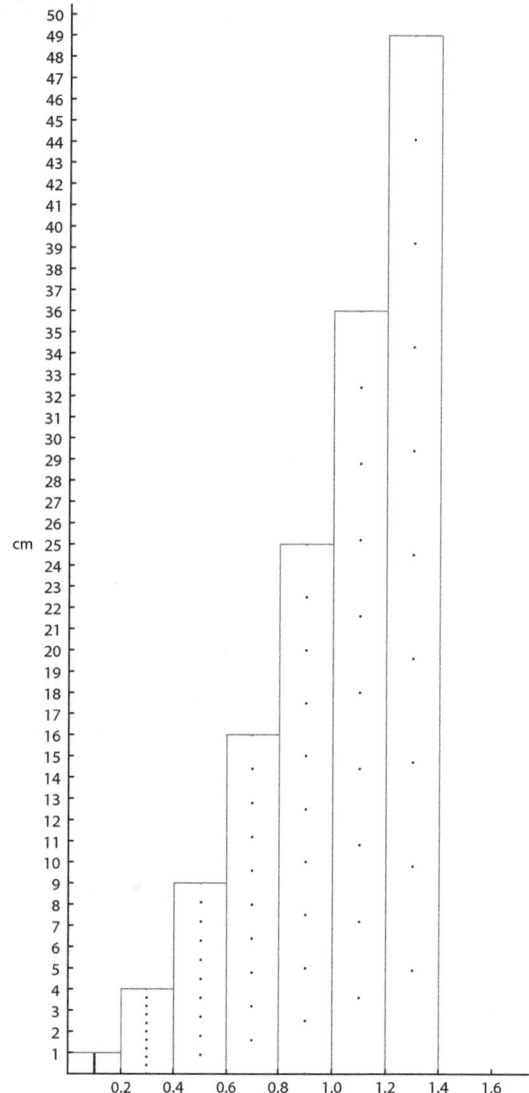

3. Triangulation method, [1] 1.25, [1] m/s^2 [1]
   $\frac{1}{2}$ base × height visible, [1] 1.5, [1] m [1]
4. Not correct. [1]
   Reason: straight-line graph represents constant acceleration. [1]

Total marks [14]

3 Forces and motion

This chapter contains investigations on:

◆ **1.3**   Mass and weight

◆ **1.5.1**   Effects of forces

◆ **1.5.5**   Scalars and vectors

◆ **1.6**   Momentum

Throughout this chapter your students will be expected to:

● draw an appropriate conclusion, justifying it by reference to the data and using an appropriate explanation
● comment critically on a procedure and suggest an appropriate improvement
● evaluate the quality of data, identifying and dealing appropriately with any anomalous results
● identify possible causes of uncertainty, in data or in a conclusion.

Practical investigation 3.1
Estimating acceleration of free fall

Planning the investigation

During this investigation students will:

● discover that the acceleration of free fall for a body near to the Earth is constant.

This investigation can be taught in conjunction with theory.

To improve accuracy, it would be helpful to agree with students beforehand whether the distance is measured from the centre or bottom of the ball.

Duration: 30 minutes

Grouping: Students should be in groups of at least 3.

Setting up for the investigation

Equipment: Stopwatch, metre rule, balls
Each group will need: metre rule, balls, stopwatch
Equipment can be left on the front bench for students to collect.

Students will record the times it takes for a ball to fall through a number of different heights. Using the equation for constant acceleration:

$$s = ut + \frac{1}{2}at^2$$

they will then plot a graph of distance against (time)^2 and use it to calculate the gradient of the line and estimate the acceleration of free fall.

Safety considerations
MH

Students should wear shoes with closed toecaps to protect their feet from injury from a falling ball.
The space below the falling ball should be clear of students before release.
Students should be advised of the correct use of equipment to prevent misuse.

Common errors when conducting the investigation

Students need to remember to allow the ball to fall freely rather than be launched. Discuss ways in which to allow the ball to do this, at the beginning of the session.

For the graph work, students are required to plot distance recorded against the square of the time. They might forget that s represents the distance travelled by the ball: remind students of this before the graph plotting exercise.

When rearranging the gradient equation, students might divide the gradient by two rather than multiply it by two to find the answer. Going through this as a worked example with the class will reduce error here.

Supporting your students

Provide students who are struggling with the graph work with a scale and a worked example for the gradient calculation. Students might struggle with the rearrangement; working through this as a class would be beneficial for less able students.

Challenging your students

Students should investigate how their results might change if they had conducted this investigation on the Moon or on another planet such as Saturn. Students should sketch the distance against (time)^2 graph for these extra-terrestrial locations and compare them with those they have drawn for their results here on Earth. A skydiver is an example of a freefalling body. Students should research the effects of the acceleration of free fall on a skydiver on each of the planets in the solar system. They should make comparisons to the terminal velocity reached on Earth.

Key discussion points for this investigation

- **Timing**: The time intervals are small but students should be able to see a difference if they use distance increments of 0.25 m. Students should practise to find a method that works for their group for indicating a time to start and stop. Should they use the same technique each time? Why?
- **Measurements**: Where will they take the distance measurement from? How will they ensure the ball is released from the same point each time? How will they ensure the stopwatch starts at the correct instant?
- **Graph**: Students will use the rearrangement of $s = ut + \frac{1}{2}at^2$ in order to calculate an estimate for acceleration of free fall. This can be discussed with the stronger candidates as an extension but is not required for the majority, as this will mimic

examination style questions. Estimates should be in the region of 10 m/s^2.
- **Error**: Where are the sources of error in this investigation? How could these be minimised? How is the reliability of the data being increased? How can the accuracy of the results be increased? How can the method be improved?

Answers to workbook questions

1   The students record their results in the table.
2   The students complete the values in their tables.
3   The students plot a graph of their results to calculate the acceleration of free fall.
4   The students draw in a line of best fit on their graph.
5   A value in the region of 20 will be acceptable for the gradient.
6   The acceleration of free fall should approximate to 10.
7   Sensible suggestion for why the value is different, for example; difficult to measure the time as the time frames were short; might not have released from the same height every time; might have misread the time on stopwatch etc.
8   Yes, a straight-line graph was obtained.
9   Use an auto release for the ball from a set point; use a fiducial (fixed point) marker; use a video recording and slow motion for a more accurate time reading.

Practical investigation 3.2
Investigating Newton's second law

Planning the investigation

During this investigation your students will:

- recall and use the relation between force, mass and acceleration (including the direction), $F = ma$.

This investigation can be taught in conjunction with the theory.

Duration: 35 minutes

Grouping: Groups of 3–4 students

Setting up for the investigation

Each group will need: trolleys, runway, three elastic bands, two pins, stopwatch, masses up to 1 kg, sticky gum, metre rule

Masses up to 1 kg should be securely attached to the top of the trolley by means of sticky gum. If it is feasible, they could also stack trolleys; note that they would require wooden pegs.

Students will perform two investigations. In the first, they alter the force being applied to the trolley by increasing the number of elastic bands used to fire the trolley. In the second, they alter the mass of the trolley. They will record the time it takes the trolley to cover a set distance of one metre and use the time taken as an indication of the trolley's acceleration.

Safety considerations

Runways should be carried by at least two people to reduce the risk of dropping them and injuring feet. Elastic bands should be placed on the pins securely and safety goggles should be worn to protect eyes.

Common errors when conducting the investigation

Using the elastic bands as a catapult to fire the trolley can sometimes cause problems for students. Demonstrate how to launch the trolley by setting up the practical on the front bench, so students can see how the equipment should be arranged. Show students how to position the elastic bands on the pins so they understand how the equipment should be used. Show them how to pull back the elastic bands to the pre-set length.

Supporting your students

Students might not understand how the time taken indicates the acceleration of the trolley. Demonstrate this by rolling the trolley freely to show that if the trolley accelerates at a higher rate it will travel a set distance in a shorter time.

Students sometimes struggle to use data to support their conclusion. Link to English and history, pointing out that a statement made in these subjects is often supported by a source or quote. The data they obtain is effectively their 'source'. If they make a statement they need to include information from this source.

Challenging your students

Students could sketch a graph showing how the relationships between force, mass and acceleration would be represented graphically. They should comment on the significance of the gradients in both instances. They can use the equation $F = ma$ to help them.

Key discussion points for this investigation

- **Variables**: What are the control variables for each investigation? Why is it important to control them? How will students control them?
- **Sources of error**: Where are the sources of error in this investigation? How will students reduce them? How could they adapt the investigation to reduce errors in future?
- **Acceleration**: How will students know if one trolley has accelerated more than another? How will this be represented in the results?
- **Reliability**: How could students make the results more reliable? If they repeat the investigation to get several readings, what do they do with anomalous results? How will they manipulate the repeat readings? How does this reduce error?
- **Conclusion**: How will they write a conclusion? What information should the conclusion contain?

1   The students record their results for increasing the number of elastic bands in the table.

2   The students record their results for increasing the mass in the table.

3   As the force on the trolley increases, the acceleration increases. This is shown in the results by the trolley covering the distance in a shorter period of time when the force is greater. (Students should use data to support this.)

4   As the mass of the trolley increases the acceleration decreases. This is shown in the results, by the trolley covering the distance in a longer period of time as the mass of the trolley increases. (They should use data to support this.)

5   Force: the mass of the trolley.
    Mass: The number of elastic bands, the distance by which the bands are pulled back.

6   Repeat the investigation three times and take an average of the results.

Practical investigation 3.3
Momentum in explosions

Planning the investigation

During this investigation students will:

- understanding the concept of momentum
- recall and use the equation
  momentum = mass × velocity, $p = mv$
- apply the principle of the conservation of momentum to solve simple problems in one dimension.

This investigation can be conducted after teaching the basic theory.

Duration: 40 minutes

Grouping: Groups of 3–4 students

Setting up for the investigation

Each group will need: metre rule, trolleys, balance, two data loggers, interrupt cards, light gates, small hammer, If there are enough trolleys and pegs, trolleys can be doubled up rather than adding masses.

If two data-loggers are used students will need to apply a direction to each of the velocities; if one data-logger is used it should apply the direction of the velocity automatically. Use clamp stands to support the light gates.

Setting up the equipment before the investigation saves time. If this is not possible, group the equipment in 'stations', leaving working space between them for the students to complete the activity.

If this isn't possible, set up the equipment on or near the front bench and allow groups of students to take turns, to use it.

In this investigation students will compare the momentum of two trolleys after they have exploded apart. The students will use kilogram masses to alter the mass of one of the trolleys, to enable them to compare their momentums as their masses differ.

If there is difficulty in obtaining the listed equipment there are two alternatives.

The quantitative alternative is to view an interactive of this experiment entitled 'Exploding Carts' in the Momentum and Collisions section of the Physics Classroom website: www.physicsclassroom.com Students can gain results from this interactive of the experiment. This allows them to still answer the questions in the Workbook and formulate a conclusion for the experiment.

Qualitatively, the principle can be demonstrated using students and skate boards. Place two skateboards touching, side by side. Ask two students of different masses to stand on a skate board each. Students should be facing one another with their hands touching. Students can then push apart from one another (explosion). The student whose mass is heavier will not travel as far as the student whose mass is smaller. This works best if there is a distinct difference in mass. Select a tall student and a shorter student, or the teacher/ teaching assistant and a smaller student, so a clear difference in initial acceleration can be noted.

Safety considerations

If students are conducting the investigation on a bench, ensure the trolleys are restrained at either end to prevent damage to the trolleys and the floor or injury to feet. Ensure that students take care when hitting the vertical rod in the trolley to reduce risk of injury to hands and fingers.

Common errors when conducting the investigation

The data-loggers will be the main source of error for the students. If they use two separate data-loggers, students will need to allocate a direction to the speeds they obtain. If speeds are significantly different, check that the interrupt card measurements are correct in the data logger.

Supporting your students

Students often muddle energy and momentum and might become confused by the negative momentum. Remind students that the negative symbol just means trolley B is moving in the opposite direction from trolley A. Students could try to formulate their own symbol for direction, if they are asked: *If you assume both momentums are positive, how will you distinguish their different directions?*

Challenging your students

Students should write a revision podcast for momentum, describing practicals they have conducted and explaining what they show them in relation to momentum and how this can be useful in everyday situations. They can do further research, for example,

relating to jumping off a skateboard at rest, ice skaters pushing away from one another.

Key discussion points for this investigation

- **Vectors**: What is a vector? Why is this significant in this investigation?
- **Reliability**: How will students ensure the data is reliable?

Answers to workbook questions

1   The students record their results in the table.
2   As velocity and momentum are vector quantities they have both magnitude and direction.
3   The momentums of trolley A and of trolley B are equal in magnitude and opposite in direction.
4   The students should repeat the investigation for each trolley mass and calculate an average of the results.

Answers to exam-style questions

1   Light gates and interrupt cards: a motion sensor: ticker tape and timer [1]
2   The mass of the trolley [1]
3   Suitable scale required [1]
    Axes labelled including units [1]
    Correct plot to $\frac{1}{2}$ square [2]
    Line of best fit [1]
    Neatness of plot and line of best fit – are they all clear [1]
4   The acceleration is directly proportional to the force applied, [1] data from graph referenced. [1]
5   Evidence of triangulation method, [1] mass approx. 500 [1] g [1] or 0.5 kg (depending on the type of trolley used)

                                    Total marks [13]

4 Turning effects of forces

This chapter contains investigations on:

◆ **1.5.2** Turning effect

◆ **1.5.3** Conditions for equilibrium

◆ **1.5.2** Centre of mass

Throughout this chapter your students will be expected to:
- explain the manipulation of the apparatus to obtain observations or measurements
- plan to take a sufficient number and range of measurements, repeating where appropriate to obtain an average value
- describe or explain precautions taken in carrying out a procedure to ensure the accuracy of observations and data, including identification and control of variables
- plan an experiment or investigation, including making reasoned predictions of expected results and suggesting suitable apparatus and techniques.

Practical investigation 4.1
The weighing machine

Planning the investigation

During this investigation your students will:
- calculate moments, using the formula:
  force × perpendicular distance from pivot to force
- apply the principle of moments to the balancing of a beam about a pivot
- apply the principle of moments to different situations
- recognise that, when there is no resultant force and no resultant turning effect, a system is in equilibrium.

This investigation should be conducted after the theory has been taught.

It would be useful to agree with student's beforehand whether or not to include the mass of the weighing pan.

Duration: 60 minutes but it can be reduced to 45 minutes if the practical equipment is already set up, as in Fig. 4.1 (below).

Grouping: groups of 4 maximum

Setting up for the investigation

Each group will need top-pan balance, metre rule, prism or fulcrum, two Newton meters, weighing pan, three small objects.

Small plastic food bags containing masses can be hooked onto the rule if no pans are available.

The small objects need to have a mass of maximum 600 g and be easy to suspend in a pan or plastic bag from the rule. Pre-weigh all objects before the investigation so that answers can be cross checked.

Setting up the equipment before the investigation saves time. If this is not possible, group the equipment in 'stations', leaving working space between them for the students to complete the activity.

If this isn't possible, set up the equipment on or near the front bench and allow groups of students to take turns, to use it.

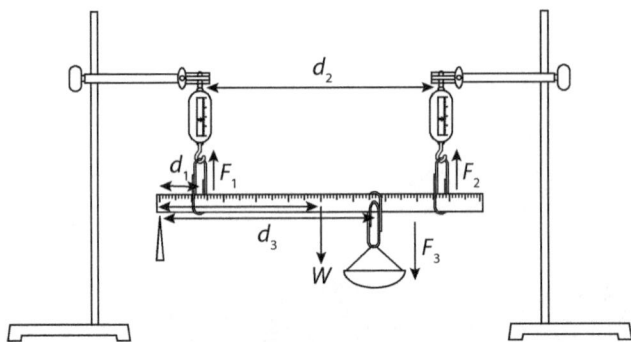
Figure 4.1

Students are asked to use the principle of moments to calculate the masses of three different objects. They will then compare their calculated measurements with the actual masses of the objects and look for ways in which to improve their accuracy.

Safety considerations

Secure clamp stands to a bench or the table to prevent toppling. Objects that are added may fall so students should wear full shoes to protect their feet from injury.

Common errors when conducting the investigation

Students will find it difficult to balance the system if they make large adjustments. One student should hold everything in place while another makes the necessary small adjustment. Then the student holding everything steady can release it. Based on what they see, they should then repeat the process until the system is balanced. Students will need patience and dexterity for this investigation.

Other errors will involve the calculation of the mass or weight. Students often muddle the two terms, even after extensive theory has been taught. Elicit the difference between the two at the beginning of the session and be explicit about what students are finding by using the moments.

As a starter, introduce the principle of moments and the conditions required for the rule to stay in equilibrium. Leave the basic equipment set up (with no additional masses added) and visible as a reference point for the investigation.

Supporting your students

Students might find the calculations in this investigation difficult. Some students struggle to identify the force providing each moment. The practical has been set up to accommodate this issue in the tabulation of results. One-to-one support might be required for the least able students.

Challenging your students

Students could use the principle of moments to construct their own mobiles. They could apply their knowledge of the principle of moments to build a mobile with two or three tiers from cards of different weights and shapes. Materials required for this additional investigation include a metal hanger, lengths of malleable wire, string, rule, tape and heavy card. Students could also investigate the use of moments in cantilever cranes, stadium roofs and mechanical levers. They could produce an A4 leaflet explaining how moments are used in order for these objects to work.

Key discussion points for this investigation

- **Setting up**: How can students ensure their equipment is set up correctly and the rule is truly balanced? Suggest ways in which they can ensure it is level, for example, by measuring the height of the rule from the floor or bench in at least two different places, or aligning the rule with a marker on the wall.
- **Accuracy**: What is accuracy? How can it be improved? For example, using a set square to align the rulers used to measure the height of the balanced rule, taking readings at eye level, improving the precision of instruments. Why is experimental accuracy important?
- **Safety considerations**: What potential hazards are there in the set up? How would students control them to reduce the risk of injury?

Practical investigation 4.2
Finding the centre of mass

Planning the investigation

During this investigation your students will:

- perform and describe an experiment to determine the position of the centre of mass of a plane lamina
- describe qualitatively the effect of the position of the centre of mass on the stability of simple objects.

This can be conducted in conjunction with the theory.

Duration: 35 minutes for the design and execution of the practical

Grouping: 2–3 maximum

Setting up for the investigation

The students are asked to design an experiment to determine the centre of mass of an irregularly shaped piece of card. They are required to know how to do this. They should be able to derive a method and equipment list, based on the theory they have learnt.

Students' equipment lists typically should include: clamp stand, cork with a nail in it, plumb-line, card shapes, hole punch, string.

The clamp stand should be secured to the bench or desk as a precaution.

Embedding the nail in the cork allows it to be fixed securely in the clamp, so that the plumb-line may be suspended from it.

The plumb-line may be a ball of modelling clay hanging from a string or a pendulum bob on string.

The card shapes must be irregular. Students can use a hole punch to make holes in thick card, then the students can make holes and suspend the cards on string.

Safety considerations

It is possible the clamp stand may topple if the card is too heavy so secure it to the bench with a clamp to prevent injury.

Students should wear full shoes and handle the pendulum bob (if used) with care as this can fall from the nail.

Common errors when conducting the investigation

Students are often disheartened when the lines do not intersect exactly. This is to be expected as it is difficult to draw the line from the plumb-line. Use this as a helpful discussion point on improvement of accuracy and refinement of method.

Supporting your students

Allow students to see exemplar methods to aid them in writing a method. If time is short, collaborate as a class to construct the correct method.

Challenging your students

Students could design and write a method to test how the centre of mass or width of the base affects the stability of an object such as a toy car.

Key discussion points for this investigation

● **Method**: How will students devise a method? How is it presented? Do they need to include a diagram of the apparatus? If so, how should this be presented and where should it be displayed?
● **Accuracy**: How will students ensure the accuracy of their results? How can they check if their results are accurate?
● **Reflection**: After conducting the experiment how would or could they improve it?

Answers to workbook questions

1 Students draw three vertical lines through different points of suspension; the lines should meet in one point.
2 Wait until the plumb-line comes to rest; use a stiffer piece of string or maybe a rod for the plumb-line; make sure the card is at eye level when drawing the lines.

Practical investigation 4.3
Tower stability

Planning the investigation

During this investigation your students will:
● describe qualitatively the effect of the position of the centre of mass (COM) on the stability of a simple object.

This investigation can be taught in conjunction with the theory.

Duration: 40 minutes (including graph and method)
Grouping: groups of 2–3 maximum

Setting up for the investigation

Each group will need: metre rule, sticky gum, blocks, ramp, protractor

The sticky gum is used to stabilise the end of the ramp, but is not necessary for the investigation as students could use a wall or the bottom of a desk.

Any blocks of uniform shape and density that can be stacked easily can be used here, for example, building blocks or pre-cut pieces of wood but they must be smooth so as not to impede topple.

The size of ramp will depend on the size of the block; trolley ramps can be used if using bigger blocks or 1 cm thick squares of wood if using smaller building blocks

Depending on the size of ramp, standard maths-kit protractors will be suitable unless the trolley ramp is being used, in which case teachers' large-sized protractors should be used.

The students are asked to design an investigation to test the statement:

> 'The higher the centre of mass of an object, the more easily it will topple on an incline.'

Students are given the equipment list and the table of results to aid their planning. Guide students towards conducting a practical experiment to test the angle at which tower blocks of various different heights topple.

Safety considerations

MH

These will depend on the size of the blocks and ramps used but, in essence, ensure students are wearing full shoes to prevent injury from falling blocks and ensure ramps are secure at one end so they do not slip and cause a trapping of fingers or hand hazard.

Common errors when conducting the investigation

Students might have difficulty in using the protractor – almost certainly, this will generate the largest errors in the investigation. Demonstrate how to use the protractor before the practical, so everyone understands.

The orientation and position of the blocks on the ramp is key in this investigation. If the way in which the students align the blocks against the foot of the ramp changes this will affect the outcome of their results. This needs to be drawn out in discussion with the students before the investigation.

Supporting your students

Some students might require extra support with reading the protractor. After a class demonstration, give one-to-one demonstrations of how to use the protractor. There are plenty of readings to take so students will soon gain confidence.

Scaling or interpreting the graph might be difficult for some students. Rectify this by revisiting scaling on a one-to-one basis or as a class. Students might obtain a slight curve in their results. This should not be focused on, as usually happens with less able students. The main aim is to observe the pattern: as the height of the COM increases, the angle of topple decreases.

Key discussion points for this investigation

- **Variables that are being tested and controlled**: Why is it important to control the width of the base? Why might the COM have an impact on the stability? Why would this be important to a manufacturer?
- **How to write a method**: What are the key things to include in a method?
- **Measuring the COM of a symmetrical object**: Refresh from previous experiment.
- **Precision and reliability**: How will students make sure the experiment is reliable? Why is this important? Why might they repeat measurements and take an average? What impact will precision have on the results? How can they alter the precision of the instrument?

- **How to read a protractor**: Discuss how to line up the baseline of the protractor, using the outer and inner scale.

Answers to workbook questions

Example method

1 Measure the height of the centre of mass of the block and record it in a table.
2 Place the block on the ramp.
3 Increase the incline of the ramp until the block topples.
4 Use a protractor to measure the angle at which it topples and record it in the table.
5 Repeat twice more and record in your table.
6 Calculate the average (mean) result.
7 Repeat steps 1–6 for a blocks with a range of heights.

Questions

1 The students record their results in the table.
2 The students plot a graph of the angle of topple against the height of the centre of mass.
3 They draw a line of best fit on their graphs.
4 Yes, as the height of the centre of mass increases the angle of topple gets smaller. The student should include key points from graph to support their answer.
5 The width of the base of the blocks. Keep the blocks in the same orientation throughout. The position of the blocks on the ramp. The starting position of the blocks on the ramp was kept the same throughout.
6 Ruler: 1 mm, Protractor: 1°
7 Smaller divisions of measurement
8 Repeat the experiment, control other variables such as the orientation of the blocks.

Answers to exam-style questions

1   1.5 cm [1]
2   2.0 cm [1]
3   15 cm; 20 cm [2]
4   Evidence of principle of moments [1]; 1.53[1];
    N [1]
5   153 [1] g [1] or 0.153 [1] kg [1]
6   The student might not have read the
    newton meters correctly, rounding errors
    in calculation; difficult to balance as a
    small object; object may not have uniform
    density. [2]
7   Take readings either side of the object or mark
    the object with a central line and align with
    the rule marking. [1]

                                   Total marks [14]

5 Forces and matter

This chapter contains investigations on:

◆ **1.5.1** Effects of forces

◆ **1.8** Pressure

Throughout this chapter your students will be expected to:
- describe or explain precautions taken in carrying out a procedure to ensure the accuracy of observations and data
- present and analyse data graphically, including the use of best-fit lines where appropriate, interpolation and extrapolation, and the determination of a gradient, intercept or intersection
- draw an appropriate conclusion, justifying it by reference to the data and using an appropriate explanation.

Practical investigation 5.1 Hooke's law

Planning the investigation

During this investigation your students will:
- plot and interpret extension-load graphs and describe the associated experimental procedure
- state Hooke's Law and recall, use and define the equation $F = kx$, where F is the force / N, k is the spring constant / N/m, x is the extension / m
- recognise the significance of the 'limit of proportionality' for an extension–load graph.

This practical can be conducted in conjunction with teaching Hooke's law.

Duration: 45 minutes including graph analysis

Grouping: 3–4 students per group, dependent on class size

Setting up for the investigation

Each group will need Clamp stand and clamp, metre rule, spring, 100 g masses, C-clamp to secure the apparatus to the bench

All clamp stands must be clamped to the edge of the workbench to prevent them from toppling.

In this investigation students will apply various loads to a spring and record its extension each time. They will plot a graph of force against extension and comment on whether the spring obeys Hooke's law.

Safety considerations

MH

Clamp stands need to be clamped to benches to prevent toppling.

Students should wear full shoes to protect their feet. Protect the floor with either a cushion or soft pad to prevent any damage from falling masses.

Students should wear goggles in case the spring snaps back.

Common errors when conducting the investigation

Students frequently calculate the extension incorrectly. They might not understand how to measure the extension or where to take measurements. Before they start the investigation, demonstrate how to take the readings and how to calculate the extension from this.

Supporting your students

Some students find it difficult to interpret the graph of results they have drawn. Offer one-to-one support or approach it as a class discussion.

Challenging your students

Students should investigate springs with higher stiffness constants and explore how this affects the results. They consider how this relates to real-life applications for springs. Students can investigate how springs are used in instruments such as seismographs, circuit breakers and shock absorbers. They should prepare and make short presentations of their findings to the class. Students can adapt their investigations to consider the relationship between load and extension when two springs are aligned in series and in parallel to each other.

Answers to workbook questions

1 Students complete the table with their own results.
2 Students plot a graph of load against extension with appropriate labels and scales.
3 Students join the points with a line of best fit.
4 Check students' graphs for anomalies.
5 A straight-line graph.
6 Yes, because it is a straight-line graph passing through the origin.
7 The graph would begin to curve.
8 The spring has been permanently deformed by the applied load.
9 The spring was still oscillating when the load was applied, not taking readings at eye level (parallax error), the ruler is not at right angles to the bench, the ruler is not aligned with the spring correctly, readings were taken from the wrong points.
10 Use a set square to ensure the rule is correctly positioned and clamp in place.

Practical investigation 5.2 Hooke's law: Investigating rubber caterpillars

Planning the investigation

During this investigation your students will:
- plot and interpret extension–load graphs and describe the associated experimental procedure
- state Hooke's law and recall and use the formula $F = kx$, where k is the spring constant
- recognise the significance of the 'limit of proportionality' for an extension–load graph.

This practical can be conducted in conjunction with teaching Hooke's law. The rubber caterpillar used in the experiment adds a fun novelty element and should be readily available - typically in gift shops at children's attractions and museums. Should obtaining rubber caterpillars prove difficult, however, then any similar long rubber item can be used instead such as a snake toy or a rubber band.

Duration: 45 minutes including graph analysis
Grouping: 3–4 students per group, dependent on class size.

Setting up for the investigation

Each group will need: clamp stand and clamp, metre rule, rubber caterpillars, 100 g masses, clamp (to clamp the apparatus to the bench), string

Rubber caterpillars or any type of long rubber toy or lace-type sweets can be used.

100 g masses should be trialled before the investigation. Most caterpillars of length 40 cm and approximately 2 cm in diameter can take up to 500g. As a safety measure, trial the maximum load before the lesson. If using lace-style sweets, use masses increasing in 10 g increments.

All clamp stands must be clamped to the edge of the workbench to prevent toppling.

Each rubber caterpillar should have string loops attached at the head and tail, tied at approximately 1 cm from the end. This enables attachment to the clamp stand and attachment to the masses.

In this investigation students will suspend various loads from a rubber caterpillar and record the extension each time. They will plot a graph of force against extension and comment on whether the rubber caterpillar obeys Hooke's law.

Common errors when conducting the investigation

Students frequently calculate the extension incorrectly. They might not understand how to measure the extension or where to take measurements. Before they start the investigation, demonstrate how to take the readings and how to calculate the extension from this.

Supporting your students

Some students find it difficult to interpret the graph of results they have drawn. Offer one-to-one support or approach it as a class discussion.

Challenging your students

Ask students who work quickly to compare their results with those of another group. If the caterpillars are indeed made of rubber they should exhibit elastic hysteresis. This occurs when, on unloading the rubber caterpillar, energy is lost to internal friction so the extension is greater than during loading. Students could compare findings and discuss the accuracy of their results, then suggest improvements for the method, to achieve more accurate results.

Students could also investigate rubber caterpillars connected in series and parallel, to see if they behave the same way as springs in series and parallel.

Suggested points for discussion

- **Accuracy**: How will students ensure they are taking accurate measurements? Suggest ideas to reduce errors for example, draw two lines on the caterpillar, one at either end, and measure original length and new length between these two points rather than from top of the caterpillar to the bottom; give a list of additional equipment such as set square, clamp stand and rule and ask students how they would use them to improve the accuracy of their measurements; discuss parallax error and its effect on the results,

- **Graph – choosing scales and plotting points**: Discuss labelling and the key elements of a graph representing direct proportionality (a straight-line graph through the origin); the significance of the limit of proportionality and where this is on the graph. Compare this to the shape of a graph for rubber and the elastic hysteresis shape and the implications of this.

- **Safety**: Why is it important to clamp apparatus to the bench? Discuss the importance of goggles and full shoe. Can they suggest any more safety issues?

Answers to workbook questions

Safety considerations

MH

Safety considerations could include:
- wearing goggles to prevent injury to eyes from any breaking caterpillars
- clamping equipment to the bench to prevent toppling
- wearing full shoes to protect feet from falling masses.

Questions

1   Students enter their results in the table.
2   Students plot a graph of load against extension with appropriate labels and scales.
3   Students draw a line of best fit.
4   The graph is not a straight line passing through the origin. No, it does not obey Hooke's law because the relationship is not directly proportional. The graph is slightly curved. Data should be used to support this answer.
5

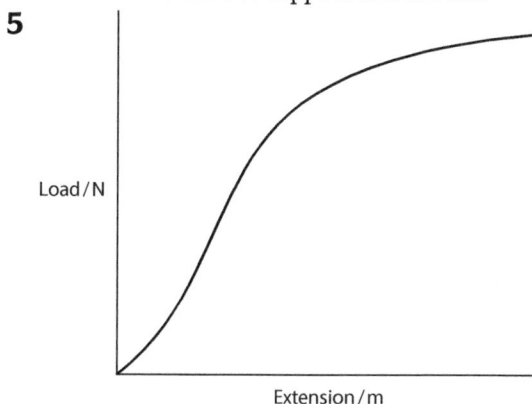

6   The extension is not directly proportional to the force applied and does not obey Hooke's law.
7   Read off the rule at eye level; used a set square and clamped metre rule; always measured the distance between the same two points. Extra care to avoid misreading the extension due to reading from incorrect place. Used a pin on the bottom of the rubber caterpillar to aid in reading the extension.
8   Misreading the extension due to parallax error. Take reading at eye level.

Practical investigation 5.3
Calculating pressure

Planning the investigation

During this investigation your students will:
- recall and use the equation $p = \dfrac{F}{A}$.
- relate pressure to force and area.

This investigation can be taught in conjunction with the theory.

Duration: 35 minutes

Grouping: Two to three per group, depending on class size

Setting up for the investigation

Each group will need: centimetre-squared paper, pencil, high-heeled shoes, stool, elephant's foot template, Newton scales

High-heeled shoes need not be worn, students draw around the regions that are in contact with the floor. Average weight of an elephant is 50 000 N.

Newton scales are used so that students can use their own weight to investigate pressure exerted by themselves wearing school shoes, someone wearing high-heeled shoes, and the stool or table. If they are reluctant to use their own, suggest they use an average weight of 700 N.

Equipment should be laid around the room as 'stations' and student groups can work their way around the room a station at a time.

Students are asked to calculate the pressure exerted by objects in given situations. They need to find the surface area in contact with the floor for themselves, a desk, a stool or chair, someone in a stiletto heel and an elephant. They will be asked to make a prediction and then compare their results to this, to formulate a conclusion for their investigation.

Safety considerations

Two students should lift the table whilst a third student slips paper under the foot, to reduce the risk of trapping fingers or dropping the desk.

Remind students of safe working in the classroom.

Common errors when conducting the investigation

Students might miscount squares. Discuss with the class useful strategies to avoid miscounting, such as marking each square as they count, or using a tally chart.

A column headed 'number of legs' has been provided in the table, to help students minimise calculation errors, since they might forget to calculate the total area in contact with the floor.

Supporting your students

Conversion from cm^2 to m^2 can be difficult for some students. Provide a table of conversion to support these students.

Converting from	To	
mm^2	cm^2	divide by 100
cm^2	m^2	divide by 10,000
mm^2	m^2	divide by 1,000,000
cm^2	mm^2	multiply by 100
m^2	cm^2	multiply by 10,000
m^2	mm^2	multiply by 1,000,000

Challenging your students

Students could investigate how pressure and surface area are related to the use of hydraulics in braking systems and machinery. They should produce an explanatory A4 leaflet about how a basic hydraulic braking system works. Students could research the effects of pressure on weather systems. Why might high pressure indicate good weather? Explain the impact of low-pressure systems on the weather we might expect.

Key discussion points for this investigation

- **Safety**: Students should write the safety considerations for this investigation. Whilst at first there might not seem to be any, students must recognise the danger of trapped fingers or injury to heads as a consequence of lifting the table to place paper underneath.
- **Accuracy – counting centimetre squares to find the area**: Discuss the inaccuracy in counting half squares and above. Why do this, knowing it is in inaccurate? How could they improve the accuracy of the count?

Answers to workbook questions

3   Students enter their results in the table.
4   Safety considerations could include:
    - care with lifting equipment such as tables
    - sensible handling of high-heeled shoes.
5   Check students' predictions against their results.
6   The stiletto provides an area 1000 times smaller than the area provided by an elephant's foot. Whilst the force of an elephant is much greater than that of a human, it is spread over a greater area and so reduces the pressure exerted on the ground.
7   Use a sharp pencil and ensure the point is held very close to the object when drawing around it. Count all squares included inside the outline.

Answers to exam-style questions

1   From the top of the spring to the bottom of the spring, or from same point on the top loop to same point on the bottom loop. [1]
2   Load / N [1]; length / m; [1] extension / m [1]
3   Suitable scale required [1]
    Axes labelled including units [1]
    Correct plot to $\frac{1}{2}$ square [2]
    Line of best fit [1]
    Neatness of plot and line of best fit – are they all clear? [1]
4   Yes, [1] straight line through the origin [1]
5   Use a set square and clamp the rule. [1]
                                        Total marks [12]

6 Energy transformations and energy transfers

This chapter contains investigations on:

◆ **1.7.1**   Energy

Throughout this chapter your students will be expected to:
- process data, using a calculator where necessary
- evaluate the quality of data, identifying and dealing appropriately with any anomalous results
- comment critically on a procedure and suggest an appropriate improvement.

Practical investigation 6.1 Gravitational potential energy

Planning the investigation

During this investigation your students will:
- identify changes in GPE that have occurred as the result of an event or process
- recall and use the expression for gravitational potential energy: GPE = *mgh*.

This practical should be conducted as part of teaching the theory.

Duration: 25 minutes

Grouping: 3–4 maximum, depending on class size

Setting up for the investigation

Each group will need: ball, balance, string, metre rule. Provide a small ball of string so students can measure the height of a staircase, for example. Alternatively, ensure that the string is long enough to measure the highest position from which the student can drop the ball. The ball must have some degree of bounce but ensure it will not damage the floor when it is dropped. Sports balls, such as those used for squash, tennis or softball, are the most appropriate.

Provide a balance with a dish on top, to keep the balls in place during weighing.

Equipment can be distributed around the classroom, with balls on the front desk, to avoid clustering. This allows you to control which group gets which ball. In this investigation students will drop a ball from five different heights and calculate the GPE in each case. They will plot a graph of GPE against height to illustrate the relationship clearly.

Safety considerations

Students should ensure the space below the 'drop zone' is clear before releasing the ball.

Common errors when conducting the investigation

Students might forget to convert the mass of the ball read from the balance from grams to kilograms, which leads to an incorrect calculation of weight. Remind students of this at the beginning of the practical. Inaccuracy in measurements might also cause errors once they have calculated the gradient. However, this can be used as a positive reflective exercise. Students can be asked to consider their investigation a step at a time, mentioning any measurements that might not have been made as accurately as possible. Students can then suggest ways to improve the method.

Supporting your students

Many students are confused by mass and weight. Start the session by reiterating the difference between them and how to calculate the weight from the mass. Leave this example on the board during the session. Calculations are the main source of difficulty in this investigation. Overcome this by doing the gradient calculation, step by step, with the group or by leaving a worked example on the board during the session.

Challenging your students

Students could research how their results might differ if the experiment were to be conducted on the Moon or another planet such as Jupiter. Students should prepare a two-minute presentation on their findings to the rest of the class.

In tennis some of the most powerful servers are very tall. Students could explain why, in terms of energy, taller players can deliver faster serves.

Key discussion points for this investigation

- **Accuracy**: How can they ensure accurate readings? How accurate do they think this method is? How could they adapt the method to make it more accurate?
- **Reliability**: How do they know their results are reliable? How could they adapt the method to ensure the results were more reliable?
- **Graph**: What relationship is displayed by the straight-line gradient? Explain proportionality. How do they select the correct scale for the graph? Gradient calculations.
- **Evaluation**: Why might the results not be equal? How would they adapt their method to ensure this error is reduced?

Answers to workbook questions

1. Students record their measurements.
2. Students plot the graph of gravitational potential energy (vertical axis) against height (horizontal axis) and draw a line of best fit.
3. As the height increases so does the GPE. This is represented by a straight-line graph with positive gradient, passing through the origin. The height and GPE are in direct proportion.
4. Look for evidence of the triangulation method. The gradient should be approximately equal to the measured mass of the ball × 10, in newtons / N.
5. Weight = measured mass × 10 / N. Differences will come from errors in measurement, such as placing the string incorrectly, misreading the length of string against the rule, any other sensible suggestion.
6. Measure a height and mark it with chalk. Release the ball from this point.
7. As the height of the drop increased the gravitational potential energy also increased.

Practical investigation 6.2
Kinetic energy

Planning the investigation

In this investigation students will:
- identify changes in KE that have occurred as the result of an event or process
- recall and use the expression for kinetic energy:
$$KE = \frac{1}{2}mv^2$$

This practical should be conducted as part of teaching the theory.

Duration: 25 minutes

Setting up for the investigation

Each group will need: chalk, metre rule or tape measure, tennis ball, newton meter or balance, stopwatch
A tennis ball or any similar sports ball can be used for the investigation.
If stopwatches are unavailable students could use phones or tablet devices. However, students are required to be able to use stopwatches effectively.
Equipment can be distributed around the classroom, with balls on the front desk, to avoid clustering. This allows you to control which group gets which ball.
Grouping: 2–4 students maximum, depending on class size
In this investigation students will roll a ball through a measured distance of 5 metres, at different rates, and calculate the speed and KE for each roll. They will plot a graph of KE against (speed)^2 to illustrate the relationship clearly.

Safety considerations

Students should ensure the ball is in contact with the floor and the rolling area is clear of other students before rolling.

Common errors when conducting the investigation

When recording the time of travel, students, unless prompted, might not record the time taken for the whole journey. At the beginning of the session, encourage students to discuss the best place to stand to get the most accurate readings.

Errors in calculation are common, due to the squaring of the speed. Remind students that the graph is of KE against the square of the speed, otherwise they will produce a curve. Some students may not fully appreciate what a curve indicates.

Supporting your students

Students will need most support in performing calculations and using the square function on the calculator. At the start of the session, run through how to use the school calculators, using an introduction activity or by writing up the process on the board. Sometimes students struggle with the concept of direct proportionality. This might require one-to-one support, to show students that as the square of the speed doubles so does the KE.

Challenging your students

Students in strong groups should use balls of significantly different masses. They can be asked to plot the graph of KE against (speed)^2 from another group onto their own axes. They compare the two graphs and draw conclusions about the effect of mass on KE. They should make reference to the gradients of the lines to ensure they have understood the principle.

Key discussion points for this investigation

- **Accuracy**: How can they ensure accurate readings? Where do they position themselves to see exactly when the ball crosses the line? Can they use slow motion video recorded on an electronic device?
- **Reliability**: Why might they want to repeat their results? Why does this improve the reliability? How would we use these repeat results? (Calculate an average.)
- **Graph**: What relationship is displayed by the straight-line graph? What does the gradient represent? Explain direct proportionality. How do they select the correct scale for the graph? Explain gradient calculations. What would a graph of KE against speed look like?
- **Evaluation**: Why might their results not be consistent? How would they adapt their method to ensure this error is reduced?

Answers to workbook questions

1 Students record their results.

2 Students calculate the square of the speed and the KE, recording their results in the table.

3 Students plot the graph of kinetic energy (vertical axis) against the square of the speed (horizontal axis) and draw a line of best fit.

4 They are directly proportional. The graph is a straight line, passing through the origin.

5 As the speed increases, the kinetic energy also increases. Data from the graph or the students' results should be quoted in support.

6 Difficulty might be in measuring time exactly. To solve, stand over the line and stop the stopwatch as the ball crosses it. Use light gates, use video recording equipment and slow motion.

7 Reliability could be improved by repeating each roll and finding the average.

8 Use balls of different masses and roll them all at the same speed, using a ramp, and release.

Practical investigation 6.3
Energy and the pendulum

Planning the investigation

During this investigation your students will:
- recognise that energy is transferred during events and processes, including examples of transfer during mechanical processes
- apply the principle of conservation of energy to simple examples.

This practical should be conducted as part of teaching the theory.

Duration: 45 minutes

Grouping: minimum of 3, ideally 4 students per group

Setting up for the investigation

Each group will need: pendulum, clamp stand, clamp to secure clamp stand, top-pan balance, light gate connected to a data-logger, 2.0 cm interrupt card, ruler Interrupt card needs to be attached to the pendulum so that it breaks the beam of the light gate.

Use a clamp to attach the clamp stand to the bench, as oscillations at a higher levels might cause it to topple. A light gate with a data-logger should be set up to record the velocity at the point at which the pendulum passes through the gate. The gate should be positioned at the pendulum's rest position. This might also need to be clamped onto the stand.

The size of the 2.0 cm interrupt card will depend on the size of the pendulum bob. It will need to be programmed into the data-logging software.

Ideally, equipment should be set up beforehand, around the edges of the room or on benches where groups can work. The practical set-up is described for the students. However, this may take too long for students to complete the investigation in one session.

In this investigation students will alter the starting height of an oscillating pendulum and use a light gate to record its velocity as it swings through its rest position. From this students will investigate the relationship between GPE and KE.

Alternatively, a qualitative investigation can be conducted using a semi-circular narrow track and a marble. If students release the marble from a certain height on one side of the track they should be able to observe the increase in speed of the marble as the KE increases and the GPE decreases. As the marble then travels up the opposite side the reverse can also be seen. The discussion points listed in this Teacher's Guide can still be used.

Safety considerations

The clamp stand needs to be clamped to the bench to prevent toppling, should the pendulum be released from too great a height or too vigorously.

Students might become animated in this investigation so close supervision of particularly lively students is advised.

Students should ensure the pendulum and interrupt card are aligned to pass through the light gate without collision, to prevent damage to the light gate.

Common errors when conducting the investigation
The data-logger needs to be set up with the correct length of interrupt card, otherwise the calculated velocities will be incorrect and the students will not be able to see that the GPE and KE are similar and the principle of conservation will not be observed. There will be some small discrepancy in values due to energy transferred to the surroundings.

Students often forget to convert mass into kilograms after weighing on the balance. Remind students about this at the beginning when discussing the equations and units used.

Supporting your students

Some students will find the manipulation of data difficult. Work through this as a class, leaving key equations on the board for these students. Demonstrate how to calculate the results from the first height and allow the class to calculate the others, allowing for one-to-one support.

Challenging your students

Students could design an experiment to investigate the effect of mass on the kinetic energy of an oscillating mass on a two-spring system.

Students could research the impact of the transfer of energy from GPE to KE in fairground rides. Is the energy completely transferred from GPE to KE? How do they try to reduce the energy loss to the surroundings?

Key discussion points for this investigation

- **Reliability**: Why does repeating results improve reliability? How would students deal with anomalies within their results?
- **Accuracy**: How can they ensure accurate readings? Where do they position themselves to see the correct value for height? How can they ensure they release from the exact same height on the repeats?
- **Graph**: Discuss choosing a scale, plotting points, lines of best fit, labelling the axes. What does a straight line imply? Why might the graph curve?
- **Evaluation**: How could they improve the investigation to overcome any difficulties in measurement?

Answers to workbook questions

1. Students record their results.
2. Students calculate and record the GPE and the KE for each height.
3. Students plot the graph of KE against GPE for each height and draw in a line of best fit.
4. As the GPE increases the KE also increases, in proportion. Students use data from the graph to support this.
5. Circle any anomalous result and omit it from the calculation of the average.
6. 1 Data-logger used to measure the velocity to a high degree of precision.
   2 Experiment repeated and the average calculated.
7. A thinner string could be used, the pendulum could be made more aerodynamic; ensure the pendulum bob does not collide with the light gate.

Answers to exam-style questions

1 0.60 m [1]

2 Ignore any anomalous results. [1] Add the values together and divide by the number of values in the addition. [1]

3 1.04, 0.92, 0.75, 0.56, 0.46 [3 marks all, 2 marks for 4 correct, 1 for 3 correct]

4 0.75 [1]

5 No, as the release height increases so does the rebound height. [1] Any example from data to support. [1]

6 Film the ball and use slow motion to see where it aligns with the rule on rebound, mark a line on the centre of the ball, this must align with the rule for the release height. Any sensible suggestion. [1]

Total marks [10]

7 Energy resources

This chapter contains investigations on:

◆ 1.7.2   Energy resources

Throughout this chapter your students will be expected to:
- identify key variables and describe how, or explain why, certain variables should be controlled
- plan an experiment or investigation, including making reasoned predictions of expected results and suggesting suitable apparatus and techniques
- select the most appropriate apparatus or method for a task and justify the choice made
- comment critically on a procedure or point of practical detail and suggest an appropriate improvement.

For both of the investigations in this chapter students will:
- describe how electricity or other useful forms of energy may be obtained from renewable energy resources
- give advantages and disadvantages of each method in terms of renewability, cost, reliability, scale and environmental impact.

These practicals can be completed as an extension to theory or may be used to display advantages and disadvantages of solar power.

Practical investigation 7.1
Solar panels

Planning the investigation

Duration: 45 minutes
Groupings: Groups of 3–4 students

Setting up for the investigation

Each group will need: rectangular trays of different sizes, measuring cylinder, thermometer, desk lamp(s), metre rule, stopwatch.

Rectangular trays should be of various sizes, coated with black paint on the inside.

The size of the measuring cylinders for water will depend on the size of the food trays being used; this will need to be determined for the session.

A desk lamp with a heated filament and an adjustable neck will be positioned over each tray or group of trays. How the equipment is set up will depend on its availability, the class size and how you wish to run the investigation. Groups can test trays one size at a time but this will take significantly longer than if the groups test three trays simultaneously. The only problem with running them simultaneously is that ideally one desk lamp per tray will be required. If this is not feasible, trays can be tested simultaneously, using one desk lamp, but students will need to consider the positioning of the lamp carefully, to ensure the intensity is uniform across the three trays. This is a good discussion point. Alternatively, trays can be placed outdoors in a sunny position if in a warm enough climate. A further investigation could be to look at comparisons between in direct sunlight and the shade.

Students will design, with guidance, an investigation that determines the impact of surface area on the time it takes for the water in the tray (representing a solar panel) to heat up. They will measure the temperature change at regular intervals, over a set time, to see which size of tray, and therefore which surface area, heats the fastest.

This practical is dependent on the food trays used, so quite a lot of preparation is required.

The trays need to be painted black inside and left to dry. The experiment will need to be trialled beforehand to determine suitable time intervals and a appropriate volume of water that will demonstrate a significant temperature rise in at least two of the trays and enable students to achieve useful results. It is suggested that the maximum time used is 25 minutes. During this time, students can write up their method and draw their equipment set up. Alternatively, a discussion can be held on the advantages and disadvantages of solar heating panels.

Safety considerations

HH

If students are using mercury thermometers, any breakages should be cleared up immediately by a member of staff and disposed of in accordance with CLEAPPS.
Any other broken glass should be cleared up immediately by a member of staff and disposed of appropriately.
Lamps should be turned off when not in use, to reduce the risk of burns.
Trays filled with water should be kept away from electricity sources to reduce risk of electric shock.

Common errors when conducting the investigation

The position of the lamp, if one only is used, is important here. If the trays do not all receive a similar intensity of light the results will be significantly skewed. Aligning the trays side by side with the lamp in an elevated position above the trays should be sufficient to overcome any problems from unequal radiation. Students will need to be reminded to take temperature readings every 1 or 2 minutes (depending on their method). Students will sometimes forget to start the stopwatch and so have to start again. To ensure that all the groups keep to time, it is suggested the class start in unison if possible.

Supporting your students

Students who are struggling with writing their method can be given an exemplar method to adapt to their experiment, by adding more detail.

Challenging your students

Ask students to adapt the food trays to reduce heat loss to the surroundings and give justification for the materials they use. For example, they may choose to add a plastic film lid to prevent heat loss from convection and evaporation, polystyrene lagging around the tray to reduce heat loss by conduction and have them all painted black. They should consider whether the trays would absorb or radiate heat from the surroundings and how this would affect the investigation.

Key discussion points for this investigation

- **Variables**: What is a suitable time frame for taking readings? Why control the volume of water/light intensity/time period/colour of tray?
- **Methodology**: How to present a method – will they do repeats? If so, what do they do with these additional readings? How will they measure the temperature change? How will they present their results?
- **Review**: How do they think the experiment went? Could they have improved the investigation in any way? What effect might this have had on their results? Were there any anomalies? How did they deal with these?

Answers to workbook questions

1. The students prepare their tables and record their data.
2. As the area of the solar panel increases, the greater the temperature rise. Therefore the greater the area, the faster it heated up. Student data should be referenced.
3. If the volume was different in each container it would affect the results.
4. The intensity of light on each solar panel will not be the same. The panel with the least intensity of light (radiation) will heat up less quickly.

Practical investigation 7.2
Solar buggies

Planning the investigation

Duration: 45–60 minutes including planning
Grouping: Groups of 4 students

Setting up for the investigation

Students are asked to draw up a list of equipment. They may list any of the following.

- Solar-cell powered buggies – these can range from the small, inexpensive toys to the larger buggies that are commercially available. They need to be able to power off and store charge. Other solar-powered vehicles may also be used to demonstrate the impact of light intensity, colour and duration.
- Desk lamps or any stable light source that students can manipulate easily.
- Stopwatch
- Metre rule or a tape measure at least 1 m long

Equipment should be laid out around the room or, if time allows, may be laid out on benches as group equipment for less able candidates.

Students are asked to design an experiment that examines the impact of duration of exposure to light on the electrical output of a buggy. This practical can also be conducted for intensity of light on electrical output if preferred. Students will be expected to; design the investigation based on the equipment at hand; identify key variables under test and to be controlled; tabulate data; comment on the graphical representation of results and suggest improvements for their experimental design.

Safety considerations

MH

The lamps should be turned off when not in use to reduce the risk of burns through contact with the bulb. Dependent on size of buggies, a soft barrier should be placed at the end of the workbench to prevent damage to buggy or floor.

Common errors when conducting the investigation

Students might forget to keep the light intensity constant or forget to turn the buggy off whilst charging. Other factors that need to be considered, that can affect the final results, are starting the buggies from the same point; whether the rule is fixed to the bench; ensuring the buggy doesn't collide with the rule or run off the workbench before it has finished its course. All solar-powered vehicles will have different capacities for converting light energy into electrical energy, so they will need to be tested before the students use them. Advice can be be given regarding periods of time to charge the buggies.

Supporting your students

Give detailed help to those who are struggling by identifying the key variables for them. As a class discussion, develop ideas for how to measure and control these variables and record them on the board, for support. Equipment can be set up beforehand so students can see how it might be used and then develop their ideas from that point.

Challenging your students

Group these students together. Ask them to consider if solar cars in tropical countries could use a smaller surface area of cells, compared to those in cooler climates, to give the same output. Students should use their findings to prepare a 2-minute presentation for the rest of the class.

Key discussion points for this investigation

- **Equipment**: What equipment will they select for the investigation? Why have they chosen this over another option (discuss precision here)?
- **Variables**: Identify the key variables under test: time taken and distance travelled, what will they need to control – light intensity (distance of light source from solar panel), colour of the light source being used? Why is this important?
- **Methodology**: How will they conduct their experiment? Will they include repeats? Why might they do this?
- **Graph**: What relationship did their data show? Were they surprised by this? Does the data support their hypothesis?
- **Review**: How do they think the experiment went? Could they have improved the investigation in any way? What impact might this have had on their results? Were there any anomalies? How did they deal with these?

- **Link in to context**: Longer exposure to the light source will produce more electrical energy.

Answers to workbook questions

1   The students prepare their tables and record their data.
2   The students use their data to draw a graph.
3   As the time for charging increases, the distance travelled by the buggy also increases. They should refer to their data.
4   Students refer to their data and results to assess whether their prediction is supported.
5   Control variables: light intensity – the distance of the lamp from solar cells was kept constant. The colour of the light was kept the same, the same bulb was used.
6   Any legitimate reason that corresponds to the students' challenge.

Answers to exam-style questions

1   26.5 °C, [1] 31 °, [1] 35.5 ° [1]
2   Any of: read at eye level to reduce parallax error; repeat results and calculate average or spot anomalous results; use a reader to check the intensity, measure the intensity; check for zero error, calibrate thermometer [2]
3   31.2; misread thermometer or any other sensible suggestion [2]
4   Correct plot to $\frac{1}{2}$ square [2]
    Line of best fit [1]
    Neatness of plot and line of best fit – all should be clear [1]
5   The greater the intensity, the greater the temperature rise ; [1] student data to support [1]

Total marks [13]

8 Work and power

Within this chapter your students will be expected to:
- describe or explain precautions taken in carrying out a procedure to ensure safety or the accuracy of observations and data, including the control of variables
- record observations systematically, for example, in a table, using appropriate units and to a consistent and appropriate degree of precision
- process data, using a calculator where necessary
- comment critically on a procedure or point of practical detail and suggest an appropriate improvement.

Practical investigation 8.1
Work done

Planning the investigation

During this investigation your students will:
- demonstrate an understanding that work done = energy transferred
- recall and use the equation $W = Fd$.

This practical can be conducted in conjunction with teaching the theory.

Duration: 20–30 minutes

Grouping: 2–4 students per group, depending on class size.

Setting up for the investigation

Each group will need: a range of masses, top-pan balance, book, metre rule.

If necessary, contact the PE department for help with a range of masses up to 1 kg, as they might have hand-held weights that can be used.

If there are no steps near the classroom or laboratory, use a thick book or plastic box. Check it will bear the weight of an adult, to ensure it does not collapse under the weight of the student.

Equipment and materials should be set out and evenly spaced around the outer edge of the classroom to avoid students clustering for equipment.

In this investigation, students will perform a circus of experiments. The aim is for them to predict and calculate which of the activities they tackle requires the most work.

1 Step-ups

Holding a mass at waist height, students step up onto the step and then down again, as in Fig. 8.1.

Figure 8.1

2 Shoulder rise

Students hold the mass in one hand and start with their arm down at their side. They raise the mass until their arm is straight above the shoulder. Return to the start position, see Fig. 8.2.

Figure 8.2

3 Static lunges

Students hold a mass in each hand, with their arms at their sides. They assume the static lunge position in Fig. 8.3. They move downwards into the lunge and return to the original position.

Figure 8.3

4 Squats

Students hold a mass in each hand with their arms at their sides. From standing they move downwards into the squat and return to the original position, see Fig. 8.4.

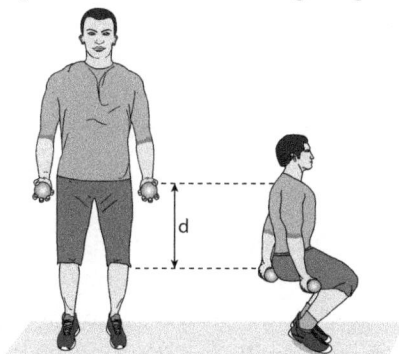

Figure 8.4

5 Bicep curls

Students start with their arm down at their side and raise the mass up until their hand is level with their shoulder. Return to start position, see Fig. 8.5.

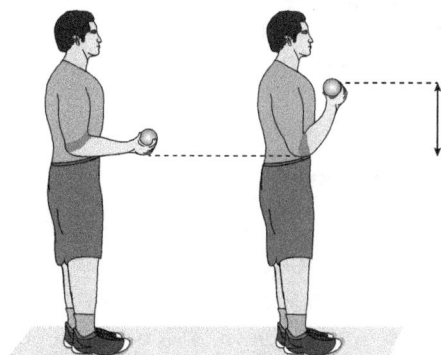

Figure 8.5

Safety considerations

HH

Demonstrate to students the correct technique for each activity, to reduce their risk of injury
Student groups should be evenly distributed around the room to reduce the risk of collision with other groups.
All students must wear shoes during the investigation to protect their feet from falling masses.
Students with health issues can restrict activities to ones they are capable of. You can also use the prepopulated data on the CD-ROM.

Common errors when conducting this investigation

Remind students that they are only considering the **upwards** motion. They will often try to calculate the total distance, including the up and down motion. Emphasise to students that they are investigating the work that is being done against gravity.
Demonstrate each of the exercises beforehand, clearly highlighting points between which they should take measurements. Students might struggle with the calculations involved. Remind them that mass is not a force. Consider reviewing this before embarking upon the practical and help the students with the equation required to calculate weight.
Remind students to convert centimetres into metres, to calculate the work done correctly. Consider reviewing this before starting the investigation, as they consider the precision of the instruments they are using.

Supporting your students

Students might not understand the difference between mass and weight and how to convert between them. Students might also struggle in changing centimetres into metres. Suggest that the students record their results in metres in the table. This should reduce the need for support here.

Challenging your students

These students recognise that the speed at which they perform the tasks has no bearing on the amount of energy being transferred. For example, whether they run or walk 200 m, the work done will still be the same, so the number of joules transferred will also be the same. This will often provoke the question: Why run? Students should investigate the benefits of running over walking, explaining in physics terms why people might opt to run rather than walk if the number of joules transferred is the same. Students should produce an A4 poster explaining their findings.

Key discussion points for this investigation

- **Theory**: Explain how force provided by students' muscles can transfer chemical energy from the muscles into kinetic energy and gravitational potential energy in either the mass that they are holding or their own bodies. Only the upwards motion is considered during the investigation because during this motion the muscles are doing work against gravity, they are transferring energy from the muscles to the object being moved. In the downwards direction however, gravity is doing work on the mass or body. This means the force of gravity is transferring energy to the object rather than the student.
- **Measurements and how they are taken**: Students should ensure that they are at eye level with the measurement point on the ruler when taking a reading, to reduce the effect of parallax error. The ruler must also be at right angles to the floor or surface when taking measurements.
- **Accuracy of measurements and how they can be improved**: For example, a fiducial marker could be used and all masses could be weighed on a top-pan balance.
- **How to record data in a table in line with precision of instrument used**: for example, headings in the table must include a title and the correct units of measurement. All answers in the table must be given with respect to the precision of the instrument used, for example, for a ruler all values measured must be accurate to the nearest millimetre.
- **Review of the method and collation of any additional ideas for improvement**: For example, demonstrate poor measurement techniques, unsafe practice, poor practical skills

Answers to workbook questions

Safety considerations

Any two which may include the following.
- Ensure that all masses being lifted above the shoulder are 1 kg or less, to reduce the chance of injury should they be dropped.
- Hazard: injury to other students when lunging or if mass dropped. Check space around them is free before starting an activity, to reduce the risk.
- Hazard: falling masses. Ensure all students have a good grip of masses or use appropriate masses for the activity to reduce risk of them dropping and causing injury to feet or other body parts.

Accept any sensible suggestions.

Table

Students should produce a table similar to the one below.

Exercise	Mass /kg	Weight /N	Distance per cycle /m	Number of cycles	Total distance moved /m	Work done/J – must use distance /m

Check all data in the table is given to the same number of significant figures, in line with the precision of the instrument used, for example, measurements taken with a metre rule with millimetre divisions must be given to 3 dp if in metres.

Questions

1 Students record their results in the table.
2 Either the lunge or the squat. Reason: they are moving the greatest weight/force through the greatest distance so will require the most energy.

3 This will depend on students' results; they need to refer to either greatest force or greatest distance in their answers.

4 Taking readings on a metre rule at eye level reduces parallax error, improving the accuracy of their measurement.

5 Students might not have travelled the whole distance and so the value calculated for work done will be too great.

6 Use a fiducial marker. Student must lunge/squat to the marker each time.

7 Top-pan balance precision is ± 1 g (will depend on balance used in class); ruler ± 1 mm

8 When the masses are moving upwards the muscles are doing work against gravity. However, when they are moving downwards, gravity is doing work on the mass.

Practical investigation 8.2
Calculating mechanical power

Planning the investigation

In this investigation students will:

- relate power to work done and time taken
- recall and use the equation: $\text{power} = \dfrac{\text{work done}}{\text{time}}$

This practical can be conducted in conjunction with teaching the theory.

Duration: 10–20 minutes (if including collation of student data)

Grouping: Students can be grouped in pairs.

Setting up for the investigation

Students are asked to compile their own lists of equipment. This will need to be discussed and obtained beforehand.

Bathroom scales may be replaced with a newton scale to be used directly for less able students.

The equipment for this investigation should be distributed evenly around the room to reduce crowding around activities. If time allows, the metre rule and stopwatches can be set out on tables and the bathroom scales lined up at the front or back of the classroom.

Some students might prefer not to weigh themselves. Tell the class that the average mass of an adult is 70 kg and that they can use this value if they wish.

Students will work out who is the most powerful member of the class based on recording the time it takes to conduct 10 squats. Students can compare their answers to formulate a conclusion about power.

Safety considerations

HH

Students should ensure they are in a space free from hazards, such as chairs or corners of tables, that may trip them or that they may encounter as they squat down. Demonstrate a safe squat technique for students, to reduce the risk of injury.

Students with health issues might be able to do a different activity such as timing bicep curls or shoulder raises, though their results will have to be considered separately.

Common errors when conducting this investigation

Students can become very excited during this practical; they might start off squatting extremely quickly and inaccurately, which will give unrealistic values up to 1 kW for power, which is a maximum for an adult male in a short burst. The aim of the investigation is to calculate the sustained power of a student doing squats, so remind them to squat at a steady rate to obtain a true value approximately 100–400 W. The main errors in this investigation will be in calculations. Remind students, at the beginning of the practical as they consider the equipment, about the difference between mass and weight.

Supporting your students

Suggest that the students record their results in metres in the table. This should reduce the need for support. Students can also be provided with a conversion table to aid them in their calculations.

Challenging your students

Students can calculate their power as they run up the stairs. Students will need to measure the height of one stair and, from this, calculate the height of the staircase. They can calculate how many squats they would need to do to generate the same amount of power.

Students should be able to calculate how long they would have to perform squats to burn off the joules in a wide range of foods. How might the number of squats differ between a more powerful and less powerful student? Students should research the impact of a hairdresser using a lower-power hairdryer over the course of one day in a hair salon. What are the time and cost implications? Why might a more powerful hairdryer not necessarily be the right option?

Key discussion points for this investigation

- **Review the method and collate any additional ideas for improvement**: for example, demonstrate poor measurement techniques, unsafe practice, poor practical skills
- **Accuracy of measurements and how they can be improved**: for example, a fiducial marker could be used, students must all travel through a set distance.
- **Measurements and how they are taken**: for example, students should ensure that they are at eye level with the point on the ruler when taking

readings, to reduce the effect of parallax error, the rule must be at a right angles to the floor or surface when taking measurements.

- **Timing small timeframes**: for example, choose a fixed value of repetitions, such as 10, to time. Divide the recorded time by this number to get the time for one repetition. This reduces errors in accuracy.

Answers to workbook questions

Equipment

Newton scale (or bathroom scale, as mass can be converted to newtons / N, as in previous investigation), metre rule, stopwatch

Safety considerations

There is risk of injury to students through over-vigorous squatting (or too many squats), losing balance or collision with bench corners. Ensure students are clear of any hazard and conduct controlled squats.

Accept any sensible suggestions.

Questions

1   Students should produce a table similar to the one below.

Name	Mass /kg	Weight /N	Depth of 1 squat /m	Total distance travelled /m	Time taken /s	Work done /J	Power /W

Students record their results in the table.

2   Answer correct, in line with experimental results. An answer that references the most energy transferred/work done.

3   No. The total work done depends on the distance travelled, not just the weight of the student. The time it takes to complete the work done will determine the power. They would not be able to determine this by looking at the students weight alone.

4   The time taken for one squat would be have too short a time period to measure it accurately. Asking a person to do 10 squats enables the calculation of an average time for each squat, reducing inaccuracy in measurement.

1   0.8 N, 2.5 N, 1.8 N, 1.2 N (1 mark awarded for correct answers, 1 for unit) [5]

2   Headings, [1] Correct units, [1]
    Correctly calculated work done [2]

Surface	Distance travelled /m	Force applied /N	Work done /J
table top	0.5	0.8	0.4
sandpaper	0.5	2.5	1.25
wooden bench	0.5	1.8	0.9
paper	0.5	1.2	0.6

3   The student should ensure the newton meter is pulling at right angles to the tub.
    The student should take meter reading at eye level.
    Accept any sensible suggestion. [1]

4   The student can attach a pulley to the tub. [1]
    As she adds masses to the pulley she can record the mass that causes the tub to move and calculate the force from here. [1]

                                    Total marks [9]

9 The kinetic model of matter

This chapter contains investigations on:

- ◆ **2.1.1** States of matter
- ◆ **2.1.2** Molecular model
- ◆ **2.1.3** Evaporation

Throughout this chapter your students will be expected to:
- draw, complete or label diagrams of apparatus
- make estimates or describe outcomes that demonstrate their familiarity with an experiment, procedure or technique
- describe or explain precautions taken in carrying out a procedure to ensure safety or the accuracy of observations and data, including the control of variables.

Practical investigation 9.1 Changes of state

Planning the investigation

During this investigation your students will:
- describe qualitatively the molecular structure of solids, liquids and gases in terms of the arrangement, separation and motion of the molecules
- interpret the temperature of a gas in terms of the motion of its molecules.

Duration: 35 minutes

Grouping: groups of 2 is ideal, 3 maximum depending on equipment and class size.

Setting up for the investigation

Each group will need: tripod, heat source, heatproof mat, gauze, 400 ml beaker, 250 ml water, thermometer, clamp stand, clamp and boss

The beaker needs to be large enough to accommodate the water. The suggested size is 400 ml. Beakers may be clamped for safety.

Data probes may be used instead of thermometers by all groups, if a class set is available, or alternatively, by just one group to show the difference in the level of precision. If a data probe is used, it will need to be clamped in position.

Tap water is suitable for this investigation.

Equipment can be distributed around the classroom, in stations, so students can collect and set it up themselves. The students are asked to make scientific observations about water being heated until it boils and evaporates.

Safety considerations

MH

Students should remain standing throughout the investigation to reduce the risk of scalding, should the water be knocked over.

Equipment should be allowed to cool before being handled, to prevent the risk of burns to students. Heatproof mats should be used underneath the heat source to prevent damage to the desk.

Common errors when conducting the investigation

Students might assume that as soon as small bubbles appear the water is boiling. These initial small bubbles are the release of air trapped within the water. True boiling of the liquid comes when larger bubbles containing water vapour rise up through the water until they are released at the surface.

Students might struggle to make accurate readings of temperature. Advise all students to stir the water to produce a homogenous solution.

Supporting your students

Struggling students will find the concept of molecules requiring enough energy to 'escape' the attractive forces of other molecules difficult. Model this, with marbles in a tray. As they shake the tray, the more energetic particles are able to escape. This also applies to molecules in a fluid, leading to evaporation. Alternatively, use polystyrene balls on a loudspeaker. As the volume (temperature) increases, the energy given to the molecules (balls) also increases, causing the molecules (balls) to move more quickly. If the volume is turned down, less energy is supplied to the molecules (balls), so they have a lower net movement.

Challenging your students

Students should be able to describe what is happening at each stage in the heating process. Ask them to explain the experiment in reverse. Students could start by drawing a cooling curve for steam as it turns into water, then ice. Their sketch should include descriptions of how the molecules are behaving at each stage.

Key discussion points for this investigation

- **Safety**: Why might it be better for students to stand rather than be seated? Why should they handle equipment with caution after use? Why might it be better to clamp the thermometer rather than let it rest in the beaker?
- **Precision**: How can students improve their precision? Precision is increased by using equipment with smaller scale divisions. Students might suggest using a digital thermometer such as a data probe, rather than an alcohol/mercury thermometer.
- **Method/theory**: Why might students wish to stir the solution? Why does the water boil when heated? How does the movement of the particles change as the temperature increases or decreases? Why does this happen? Why does the temperature remain constant when boiling? Where is the energy going? Do they think this would be the same in reverse, for example,

if the steam was cooling to form a liquid? How are the bubbles in boiling water different to warming water?

- **Sketching graphs**: What is important to include in a sketch? How is plotting a graph different from sketching a graph?

Answers to workbook questions

1. Students record their results in the table.
2. Small bubbles start to rise, as air escapes, then larger bubbles form.
3. Large bubbles, steam escapes from the surface, temperature close to 100 °C. At 100 °C; it stays the same.
4. The temperature remains constant.
5. Students sketch a graph of temperature against time.

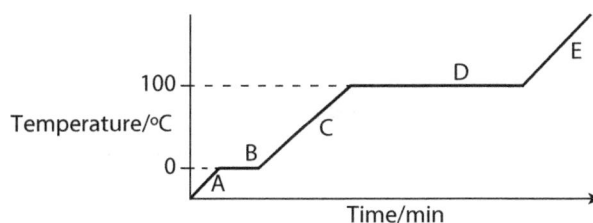

6. Energy is being absorbed by molecules during this time which causes the molecules to move more quickly thus increasing the molecules' kinetic energy.
7. There are two horizontal sections in the graph. At these points the ice/water are changing state. Energy is still being provided but is being used to break the bonds between molecules so that the ice can melt into water and the water can change into vapour that leaves the liquid. During this time the temperature remains constant.
8. The temperature of the water might not be consistent throughout.
9. Choose a thermometer with smaller scale divisions or a digital thermometer with a higher degree of precision.

Answers to exam-style questions

1   Heat source [1], beaker [1], tripod [1]
2   Always stand when heating the water to avoid scalds, clamp thermometer so it doesn't topple the beaker; take care when handling the apparatus after use [1 for each valid consideration, total of 2 marks available].
3   Suitable scale required [1]
    Axes labelled including units [1]
    Correct plot to $\frac{1}{2}$ square [2]
    Neatness of plot and line of best fit – are they all clear? [1]
4   As the temperature increases, the amount of sugar dissolved also increases; [1] data used to support. [1]
5   As the temperature of the water increases, the net kinetic energy of the water molecules also increases. [1] This means that the water molecules will collide more frequently with the sugar, causing it to break up faster, thus dissolving more easily. [1]

                                    Total marks [14]

10 Thermal properties of matter

Throughout this chapter your students will be expected to:
- describe or explain precautions taken in carrying out a procedure to ensure safety or the accuracy of observations and data, including the control of variables
- identify possible causes of uncertainty, in data or in a conclusion
- draw an appropriate conclusion, justifying it by reference to the data and using an appropriate explanation.

Practical investigation 10.1 Thermal expansion of solids

Planning the investigation

During this investigation your students will:
- appreciate how a physical property that varies with temperature may be used for the measurement of temperature, and state examples of such properties.

This can be taught…

Duration: 30 minutes

Grouping: 2–3 students per group, depending on class size and availability of equipment.

Setting up for the investigation

Each group will need: tripod, gauze, heat source, beaker, water, ink, clamp stand, clamp, boss, soda glass test tube, bung with capillary tubing to fit test tubes, laboratory glass test tube, thermometer.

A water bath preset to 60 °C could be used rather than using a heat source for heating.

The soda glass test tube and the laboratory glass test tube should both be 75 mm by 12 mm.

Use a bung with capillary tubing to fit the test tubes.

Clamp stand, clamp are optional, to be used for securing the test tubes in the beaker so students do not have to handle them.

Equipment should be evenly distributed around the edges of the classroom to avoid crowding when students are collecting it. In this investigation students are asked to observe what happens to a soda glass test tube fitted with a bung and capillary tube and a laboratory glass test tube when they are placed in hot water. Students should be able to explain that the expansion of the solid causes the apparent drop in fluid level.

Safety considerations

MH

All heating equipment should be allowed to cool before being handled. If time is restricted, students must wear safety gloves if they need to handle hot equipment.

Common errors when conducting the investigation

Students sometimes fail to notice that, initially, the volume of the fluid appears to decrease and so do not realise that the glass from which the tubes are made expands. This can be seen to varying degrees, depending on the type of glass from which the tube is made. If students do not spot this initial drop or notice a marked difference between the tubes then they will be unable to formulate a detailed conclusion.

Supporting your students

Students can be given a diagram of what happens for each of the two tubes and thermometer. In a group, they could be asked to come up with reasons why they think the volume might seem to decrease then suddenly increase. This could be discussed one-to-one.

Challenging your students

In the Galilean thermometer, sealed balls of coloured fluid indicate the temperature of the room in which the thermometer is placed. Students should produce an A4 poster explaining how the thermometer works. They should refer to temperature, fluid expansion and density.

At the beginning of a Formula-1 race, drivers take the cars on a warm-up lap. Why might a warm-up lap be required for both the engine and the tyres? Students research the physics behind this and prepare a short presentation to the class.

Key discussion points for this investigation

- **Safety**: What risks can the students see? How can they adapt their method to reduce this risk?
- **Recording observations**: How will students record observations? What things must be documented? Would it be appropriate to use diagrams?
- **Interpreting data**: Why might the volume of fluid appear to reduce when the test tube it is first placed in the hot water? Where else might the energy be going? What does expansion imply in terms of molecules? How has the spacing between the particles changed in a substance that is heated? What would a bigger drop in level imply about the materials' ability to absorb heat?

Answers to workbook questions

1. The fluid volume appears to decrease.
2. The fluid volume appears to decrease more than in the thermometer.
3. The fluid volume appears to decrease less than in the thermometer.
4. The glass surrounding the fluid expands and so the internal volume of the tube increases, giving the impression that the fluid has decreased in volume.
5. The laboratory glass test tube has expanded less than the soda glass test tube.
6. From the observations, the fluid in the soda glass tube seems to dip the most initially. The glass from which this is made expands more, compared to the glass of the laboratory glass tube. The expansion can be measured more accurately by marking the starting position of the fluid in the capillary tube and then marking the point to which it drops.

Practical investigation 10.2 Measuring the specific heat capacity of aluminium

Planning the investigation

During this investigation your students will:
- relate a rise in the temperature of a body to an increase in its internal energy
- describe an experiment to measure the specific heat capacity of a substance
- recall and use the equation change in energy $= mc\Delta T$

Duration: 45 minutes

Grouping: 2–3 students per group, depending on class size and availability of equipment.

Setting up for the investigation

Each group will need: 1 kg block of aluminium, insulating material, 50 W heater, thermometer
The aluminium block should be lagged with an insulating material and should be placed on a heatproof mat.
Use a heater with a known power rating – 50 W is preferable but not essential. Students are asked to measure the starting temperature of the aluminium block. They will then place a heater into the centre of the block and record the temperature at regular intervals. If an aluminum block is not available, it is possible for students to design an investigation to calculate the specific heat capacity of water. Students should follow the same procedure using 0.5kg of water in a beaker and an electric heater of known power rating.

Safety considerations

MH

Students should allow the block to cool before handling it. They should use tongs if they need to handle the block before it has cooled.

Common errors when conducting the investigation

Before they start the investigation, remind students that they will need to record the starting temperature of the block, to be able to calculate a rise in temperature. Lagging should be provided for the block, to reduce heat loss, otherwise results might not be accurate enough.

Supporting your students

Many students will struggle with the maths calculation in this investigation. It may be useful to go through this with the class as a whole or ask more able students to team up with less able students to assist them in the calculations.

Challenging your students

Students should discuss whether the method they have used would be suitable for measuring the specific heat capacity of materials such as wood and cloth. They should then research how the materials industry determines the specific heat capacity of non-metals.

Key discussion points for this investigation

- **Safety**: Why should students not handle the heater or block during the investigation? How should it be handled once the experiment is over?
- **Accuracy**: Discuss the other variables that students need to control. How can they ensure accurate measurements? What might affect their results?
- **Method**: What measurements will they take? How regularly are they going to take temperature measurements? How will they calculate the energy supplied to the block?
- Discuss the two method options.
  Method 1: Take initial reading of the block and then again after a fixed period of time, for example, 10 minutes (to be able to calculate the energy supplied using the power rating).
  Method 2: Take readings over regular intervals and calculate the gradient at a point on the line of best fit on a graph of temperature against time.

Method

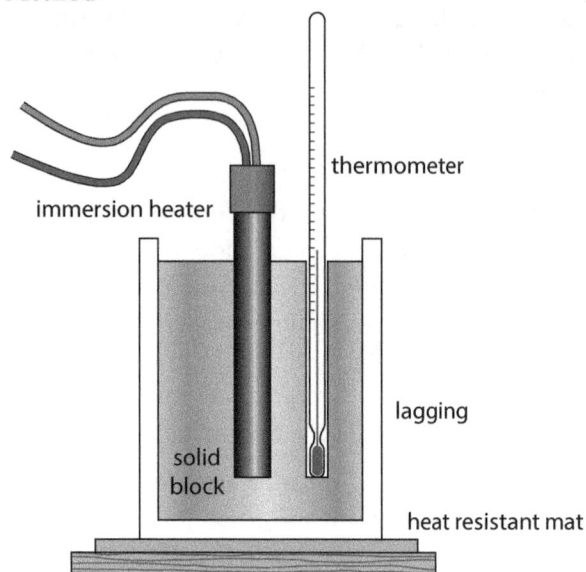

1 Weigh the block.
2 Measure the energy supplied to the block (from a 50 W heater for a fixed period of time say 5 minutes).
3 Record the temperature change.

Questions

1 See CD-ROM for results.
2 904 J/kg °C
3 Aluminium. The aluminium will require more energy to increase its temperature and so will transfer less energy to the outside of the building.
4 Better lagging to prevent heat loss, reading the thermometer at eye level, taking more regular readings.

Practical investigation 10.3
Measuring the latent heat of fusion of ice

Planning the investigation

During this investigation your students will:
● use the terms 'latent heat of vaporisation' and 'latent heat of fusion' and give a molecular interpretation of latent heat
● describe an experiment to measure specific latent heats for ice
● recall and use the equation: energy= ml

This can be taught after the basic theory of latent heat.

Duration: 35 minutes

Grouping: 2–3 per group, depending on class size and availability of equipment.

Setting up for the investigation

Each group will need: 0.1 kg ice, stopwatch, beaker, balance, thermometer, 50 W heater

A polystyrene cup is an optional alternative. Students can use the beaker but results might have significant difference to the accepted value due to energy loss to the surroundings.

Equipment should be evenly distributed around the edges of the classroom to avoid crowding when students are collecting it. Students are required to measure the mass of the ice used and calculate the energy supplied to the ice by recording the time taken for the temperature of the ice to start to rise. From this, students can then calculate the latent heat of fusion of ice.

For classrooms in warmer environments, results may be distorted by some energy being provided from the environment heating the ice. One way around this is to allow the ice to melt without the heater for a fixed time.

Safety considerations

Students should remain standing to reduce the risk of scalds from hot water.

Students should be reminded not to eat the ice provided in the laboratory, in case of cross contamination.

Common errors when conducting the investigation

The main source of errors for this investigation comes from students incorrectly taking temperature measurements before or long after the ice has melted. Students should be reminded to stop the stopwatch **as soon as** they notice a change in the temperature of the melted ice water.

Supporting your students

Struggling students will require assistance with the theory relating to the calculations required. This may be offered to a whole group or as one-to-one support. Completing and displaying a worked example on the board should help students to work out how to do it for themselves. Alternatively, they could use a joulemeter to determine the energy supplied.

Challenging your students

These students could design an experiment to measure the latent heat of vaporisation of water. Their method should include:

● the equipment required
● a diagram of the experimental set up
● how to conduct the practical
● the measurements they will take.

Students could research the effect of latent heat on the production of weather patterns and storms.

Key discussion points for this investigation

● **Theory**: The energy required to break down the bonds between the particles in a solid, for it to form into a liquid, will be equal to the energy given out by bonds as they form when a liquid turns into a solid. Why is energy required to break the bonds? How would this affect the temperature of the ice?
● **Accuracy**: How can students improve the accuracy of their measurements of temperature?
● **Method**: How could they improve their method to reduce the heat loss? How could they make the results more reliable? How have they made them reliable in this investigation?

Answers to workbook questions

1 Students record their results in the table.
2 Students calculate the energy supplied.
3 Evidence of using latent heat of fusion = energy supplied/mass. Values should be in the region of 330 kJ/kg.
4 Evidence of students adding their three results for latent heat of fusion and dividing by 3. It should approximate towards 334 kJ/kg.
5 Students should compare their result to the stated value and comment on how they compare and their accuracy.
6 Students should state whether or not their value supports their initial prediction.
7 Additional energy loss to the surroundings, incorrect measurement of temperature, incorrect measurement of mass, any sensible suggestion.
8 Additional lagging around the polystyrene cup, a lid for the cup.

1   The table headings

No. of turns / n	Starting temperature / °C	Final temperature / °C	Temperature rise, θ / °C	Specific heat capacity of lead J/kg/°C
20	22.8	24.3	1.5	134
30	22.4	24.7	2.3	130
40	21.1	24.2	3.1	136
50	20.9	24.9	4.0	125

Headings: two correct; [1] all four [2]

2   Temperature rises: two correct; [1] all four [2]

3   1 mark per correct answer [4]

4   The mean of student's results is 134 J/kg/C. This result is similar to the accepted value of 128J/kg/C. The value for the students results is slightly higher [1]. This may be due to the student incorrectly measuring the mass of the lead shot, energy being transferred to the tube as heat or any other sensible suggestion [1]

5   Lead is poisonous so should be handled carefully. [1]

Total marks [11]

11 Thermal (heat) energy transfers

This chapter contains investigations on:

◆ **2.3.1** Conduction

◆ **2.3.2** Convection

◆ **2.3.3** Radiation

◆ **2.3.4** Consequences of thermal (heat) energy transfer

Throughout this chapter your students will be expected to:
- explain the manipulation of the apparatus to obtain observations or measurements, for example:
  - plan to take a sufficient number and range of measurements
  - identify key variables and describe how, or explain why, certain variables should be controlled
- plan an experiment or investigation, including making reasoned predictions of expected results and suggesting suitable apparatus and techniques.

Practical investigation 11.1
Conductors of heat energy

Planning the investigation

During this investigation your students will:
- describe experiments to demonstrate the properties of good and bad thermal conductors.

This investigation can be taught in conjunction with theory.
Duration: 60 minutes including graphical analysis and questions.
Grouping: 4 students per group is ideal.

Setting up for the investigation

Each group will need: 4 beakers, a sheet of each material, elastic band, hot water, thermometer, stopwatch
The materials could be wool, felt, aluminium foil, cotton – in

fact any materials can be used that have different insulating properties. Materials from around the home, such as fibre glass cladding, polystyrene cladding, could also be used. String could be used, instead of the elastic band, to tie the material around the beaker.

Use boiling water from a kettle. This quickly cools to approximately 85 °C, a good starting temperature for the investigation.

Equipment should be evenly distributed around the edges of the classroom to avoid crowding when students are collecting it.

The boiling water is best supplied by the teacher. For speed, keep two or three kettles filled and boiling at any one time. When students have completed their methods and constructed their tables of results, they can be supplied with four beakers-worth of water. Pour water at the desk – no beakers should be carried.

Students are asked to design a practical to investigate which of the materials is the best insulator, from a choice such as wool, felt, aluminium foil and cotton. Students have been given an equipment list and are expected to write a method, construct a table of results and consider the safety implications.

Safety considerations

MH

Students must conduct the investigation standing to reduce the risk of scalding.

Beakers of water must be left to cool before being handled. If fibreglass is being used, gloves must be worn to prevent glass splinters.

Common errors when conducting the investigation

Students will try to work with one beaker at a time, which is extremely time consuming. Advise students to run the four beakers concurrently. A group of four students shouldn't find this taxing as each can take a temperature reading when the stopwatch reaches 0, 2, 4, 6, 8 and 10 minutes. Between taking readings, students can be recording the results of the other beakers in their group. This investigation can be made simple for the students if they arrange all four beakers in a row, with the thermometer already in place, and they pour the water straight into the beakers up to the 250 ml mark for example.

Supporting your students

Students will struggle to plot the four graphs on one set of axes, as they will not know how to organise themselves. Suggest students plot all the points of one material first and draw in the curve of best fit, then do the second, and so on. They should use a key to identify the materials.

Challenging your students

Students can design a quantitative investigation to test the thermal conductivity of metals. They should include:
- a diagram of the experimental set up
- how to conduct the practical
- the measurements they will take
- how they will make sure they have accurate results.

Key discussion points for this investigation

Variables: Independent – time; dependent – temperature drop; control variables – volume of water, starting temperature of water (this may be tricky), size of beaker, material of beaker, thickness of beaker (this will be impossible to control but still worth discussing), lid made of the same material for all the beakers, time over which the temperature drop is measured.
Method: How will students observe a drop in temperature? How many temperature readings will be required, to plot a suitable graph or recognise a relationship? How will they structure their method?
Safety: What issues can the students see? How will they reduce the risk of scalding?
Recording data: How will they construct the table?

What will the headings and units be? Do they need separate tables for each material?
Graph: How will they plot four graphs on one set of axes? Discuss scaling, labels, units, line of best fit, key to identify each curve. What is the importance of the gradient? What does it represent?

Safety considerations

MH

Stand up whilst conducting the investigation to prevent scalds to the skin should the beaker be knocked over. Allow equipment to cool before handling to prevent burns and scalds.

Answers to workbook questions

Table for recording data

Time /s	Temperature / °C
0	
30	
60	

Questions

1   Students should systematically record their results in a table relevant to their method.
2   Students should construct a temperature against time graph. Students should plot their results one fabric at a time and then fit in a line of best fit. The final graph should have four cooling curves, one for each material.
3   The students identify the material that enabled water to cool most slowly and suggest a reason, such as it being a non-metal with fixed atoms.
4   A non-metal has no free electrons to transfer thermal energy quickly.
5   The volume of water was kept consistent at 250 ml using a measuring cylinder.
6   Any two from: Size, thickness and material of beaker – used the same type of beaker
    Environment – beakers placed in same position in the room
    Time – all recorded at the same time.
    Loss of heat by convection – lid of the same material on each beaker
    Conducted repeats and took an average.

Practical investigation 11.2 Heat transfer by convection

Planning the investigation

During this investigation your students will:
- recognise convection as an important method of thermal transfer in fluids
- relate convection in fluids to density changes and describe experiments to illustrate convection.

This practical can be conducted as an exploratory investigation on convection. The explanation section can be completed after the theory is taught.

Duration: 20 minutes

Grouping: ideally students work in pairs, depending on class size and equipment availability.

Setting up for the investigation

Each pair of students will need: a sheet of card. a pair of compasses, ruler, scissors, string, clamp stand, clamp and boss, heatproof mat, 2 tea light candles

Instead of using compasses, students could draw round the base of a large circular object for the outline. Distribute the equipment evenly around the classroom but keep tea light candles and matches on the front bench for safety reasons. Students can collect the candles one at a time so they can be counted out and in. Students are asked to observe what happens to a paper spiral suspended above a heatproof mat, on which there is nothing, then one tea light candle and finally two tea light candles.

Safety considerations

MH

Paper near a lit candle could catch fire so ensure it is suspended well above the top of the flame.

Allow the candles to cool before handling them, to prevent scalds from hot wax.

Scissors and compasses should be held correctly when they are transported, to reduce the risk of stab injuries.

Common errors when conducting the investigation

Students sometimes forget to leave a central disk of diameter of about 2.5 cm from which to suspend the card. This makes it difficult for the disc to rotate so the students will not be able to observe its motion clearly.

Supporting your students

Use the demonstration of marbles in a flat tray to represent the particles in the gas. If you supply more heat energy to the particles (jostle the tray more vigorously) the particles move more quickly. So, if the gas particles above the tea light candles move more quickly they will collide with the paper more frequently, causing it to rotate faster.

Challenging your students

Students could design a leaflet that explains how convection currents in refrigerators work; they should explain why the freezer compartment is placed at the top of the standard kitchen fridge.

Key discussion points for this investigation

Safety: What safety issues can the students identify? How will they reduce their risk of injury?

Theory: Why is the hot air causing the paper to spin? Why might two candles cause it to rotate faster? If the heat energy provided to the particles is increased, how does their behaviour change?

Answers to workbook questions

Safety considerations

The card should be positioned at least 2 cm above the flame to reduce the risk of the card catching fire. Candles should be allowed to cool before being handled

Questions

1 Without a candle: turns in different directions, no pattern in movement
   With one candle: turns clockwise at a constant rate
   With two candles: turns clockwise at a constant rate, more quickly than with 1 candle

2 As the air is heated the particles in it gain more energy, causing an increase in the spacing between them. This causes the air to become less dense. The unheated (cooler) air contains particles that are more closely packed together, meaning this air is more dense. This pushes the warmer air upwards, which causes the spiral to rotate.

3   As the temperature increases with a second candle, the air particles gain more energy and move faster as a result. As the particles move more quickly upwards, the collisions of the air particles against the paper becomes more frequent, causing it to spin faster.

Practical investigation 11.3 Heat transfer by radiation

Planning the investigation

During this investigation your students will:
- describe the effect of surface colour (black or white) and texture (dull or shiny) on the emission, absorption and reflection of radiation
- describe experiments to show the properties of good and bad emitters and good and bad absorbers of infra-red radiation.

This investigation can be taught in conjunction with the theory.

Duration: 20 minutes

Grouping: 2–4 students per group, depending on the number of radiant heat sources and class size.

Setting up for the investigation

Each group will need: a radiant heat source such as a radiant heater, high wattage light bulb or electric heater, a white screen with hole and stand, very thin aluminium leaf, vegetable black, paint brush.

Advise students not to put the radiant heat source up close to the screen – 5 cm away from it should be sufficient. Aluminium foil cannot be substituted for aluminium leaf, since it has a higher thermal capacity and therefore may cause damage to the thermometer.

Black paint can be used instead of vegetable black.

A beaker containing methylated spirit can be left on the front bench for cleaning the brushes.

Equipment should be evenly distributed around the edges of the classroom to avoid crowding when students are collecting it. Students are asked to compare the heat energy absorbed from a radiant heat source by silver aluminium leaf and blackened aluminium leaf placed on the bulb of a thermometer.

Safety considerations

MH

Students must use tongs or wooden pegs to handle the thermometers, to reduce the risk of burning. Emphasise this to the students at the beginning and during the investigation.

Students must allow the heater to cool before handling it, to reduce the risk of burning.

Methylated spirit should be kept on the front bench away from naked flames.

Common errors when conducting the investigation

Students might struggle to apply the aluminium leaf evenly. If the thermometer is made moist before applying the aluminium leaf and the leaf is blown into place, this makes application easier. Students should ensure they place the thermometer, covered with the aluminium leaf, as close to the hole in the screen as possible without touching. The radiant heat source should also be in line with the hole to ensure radiation is reaching the thermometer.

Supporting your students

Discuss common uses of the materials with which students can identify, to explain the results or the principle. For example, why do they wear light bright clothes in the summer and darker clothes in the winter? When cooking, why put the shiny side of the foil against the meat? Why are houses in hot countries painted in bright colours?

How to stretch and challenge more able students

Students should produce an information leaflet on how heat loss is reduced in homes. They should provide examples of how heat loss is reduced through, convection conduction and radiation illustrating how each of the materials used works.

Key discussion points for this investigation

- **Safety**: What implications can the students see and how will they reduce the risk? Why limit the time for the hand next to the hole?
- **Theory**: Why might the silvered surface be a poor absorber of heat? The black is a good absorber of heat. How does this relate to ability to emit heat?
- **Evaluation**: How could they adapt the practical to get numerical data?

Answers to workbook questions

1   Students record their results in the table.
2   The blackened aluminium leaf absorbs more heat energy as there is a bigger increase in temperature in this thermometer. Students should make reference to their prediction.
3   Black materials that are good at absorbing heat energy are also good emitters. A black heater will emit more heat into the room.
4   Yes the results are valid. This is because the method accurately measures the amount of heat energy absorbed by the different coloured materials. Variables such as the distance from the radiant heat source and surface area exposed were kept controlled so as not to impact the results.

Answers to exam-style questions

1   The black matt surface is the best absorber of heat. [1] It has the greater increase in temperature over the time period. [1]
2   Award 1 mark for any valid answer; for example:
    Allow cans to cool before repositioning or packing away.
    Allow heater to cool before moving. [1]
3   Various options are available, students should supply three, award 1 mark for each.
    Distance from the heat source to the cans.
    Volume of water.
    Material the can is made from.
    Starting temperature. [3]

Total marks [6]

12 Sound

This chapter contains investigations on:

◆ **3.4** Sound

Throughout this chapter your students will be expected to:
- describe the outcome of their practical and show that they have understood the investigation.
- plan to take a sufficient number and range of measurements, repeating where appropriate to obtain an average value
- draw an appropriate conclusion, justifying it by reference to the data and using an appropriate explanation

Practical investigation 12.1 Measuring the speed of sound

Planning the investigation

During this investigation your students will:
- describe an experiment to determine the speed of sound in air
- describe how the reflection of sound may produce an echo.

This investigation can be taught in conjunction with theory.

Duration: 20 minutes.

Grouping: Ideally, students work in pairs.

Setting up for the investigation

Each pair will need: stopwatch, two blocks or hands, a reflective surface such as, a wall or large metal sheet, metre rule

Students are asked to produce a sound towards a reflector and record the time it takes for the echo to return. From this, students will be asked to estimate the speed of sound in air.

Safety considerations

If students are using blocks, ensure they hold them in such a way as not to trap fingers when clapping them together.

Common errors when conducting the investigation

Students might have difficulty in distinguishing the echo. Perform an initial demonstration so that students can recognise what the echo sounds like. If students still struggle with achieving the echo, do the investigation as a whole class, or with the teacher leading a small group.

Supporting your students

Students can struggle to understand that the distance travelled by the echo is double the measured distance. Talking through this as a class and illustrating with a diagram can help.

Challenging your students

Pierre Gassendi, in 1635, first determined the speed of sound. Students should research his method and comment critically on its design. They should suggest improvements Gassendi could have made to the investigation in order to achieve a more reliable result.

Key discussion points for this investigation

- **Reliability and accuracy of results**: Why might taking an average of several readings be more reliable? Why should students record the time over ten echoes rather than one? Would standing further away from the wall improve accuracy?

- **Theory:** An echo is produced by the sound reflecting at a surface. What implications does this have for calculating the speed of sound, given students' measurements?
- **Method:** When should the timer start? When should it be stopped? Why is a regular rhythm important? What impact will an irregular rhythm have on the results? How could this be rectified?

Answers to workbook questions

1 Between 20–50 m measured to the nearest cm.
2 They draw up a table to complete the investigation.

Attempt	Time taken for ten claps /s	Time taken for 1 clap /s
1		
2		
3		
average		

3 Evidence of speed = (distance from surface × 2)/ time taken for 1 clap. Results should be in the region of 300 m/s.
4 Yes – The time for 10 claps was recorded to reduce the error in the timing. No – it was difficult to distinguish the echo and so the timings recorded were inaccurate or another sensible suggestion that supports their argument.
5 Any discrepancy in centimetres in relation to the distance will be smaller over a large distance, for example, 5–10 m, than over a shorter distance so it can be neglected in this calculation.
6 When the blocks are being clapped at a steady rate, it is more accurate to record the time taken for a larger number of claps. This is because any inaccuracy in starting and stopping the stopwatch is much smaller over a longer time period than a shorter one.

Practical investigation 12.2 Sound through different substances

Planning the investigation

During this investigation your students will:
- show understanding that a medium is needed to transmit sound waves
- show understanding that the arrangement of the particles in a medium determines how quickly the sound will travel through it.

This investigation can be taught in conjunction to or as an introduction to the theory.

Duration: 20 minutes
Grouping: Ideally, students work in pairs. Allow each student to experience the practical.

Setting up for the investigation

Each pair will need: wire coat hanger, two pieces of string or plastic film strips, metal rod.
Students can be asked to provide the wire coat hangers. Any coating will need to be stripped back to leave just the wire frame. for the full effects to be heard.
Plastic film strips can be used instead of the string.
Any metal instrument, such as a fork or spoon, can be used as a metal rod.
The equipment can be organised into three piles at the front of the classroom. Separate the piles to prevent crowding when students collect equipment. Students are asked to tap the frame with the metal rod and record their observations. Then they are asked to repeat the experiment, but this time with their fingers in their ears. This should produce a louder sound in their ears. Students can then deduce that solids are better transmitters of sound than gases are.

Safety considerations

The pointed ends of the hangers should be covered with blue tack to avoid stabbing injuries.
Students must wind the string so that is it comfortably tight around their fingers, to prevent bruising to the hands.

Common errors when conducting the investigation

If the students wrap the string around their index fingers too loosely, they will not hear the sound as loudly. They should wind the string tight around the fingers, but not so tight that it is uncomfortable. If students struggle to receive the sound, there are two demonstrations that can be performed to achieve the same effect.

- Students can use a tuning fork: they hit the desk with the tuning fork and observe what they hear. They repeat this, hitting the desk with the tuning fork and then touching the tuning fork to something solid, such as their arm or the bench again.
- Another useful demonstration uses the motor and sound mechanism of a music box. When the motor is wound and run in the air, little sound is heard. If the motor is run when pressed against a solid surface, such as a desk or bench, it is much louder. The vibration from the music box is transferred through the more densely packed particles of the solid and then to the surrounding air from the large contact surface of the solid.

Supporting your students

Students can be used to model what is happening on a molecular level. Ask six students to arrange themselves side by side in a line, as if they were atoms in the solid. Give them a piece of string as long as the line they have formed. Each student should hold onto the string. The first students should vibrate the string. When the vibration reaches the second student they should then add a vibration; this continues down the line. Ask students to mimic the widely spaced particles in a gas. It should be immediately clear that because the particles are so spaced out and constantly moving, it is difficult for one particle even to come into contact with the first particle to 'receive' the vibrations so the transmission of sound is lost.

Challenging your students

Students should design a quantifiable investigation that tests sound transmission in all three media and a vacuum. They should include:

- the measurements they will take
- the variables they will control
- how they will conduct the investigation
- safety measures
- a predicted outcome with reasoning.

Key discussion points for this investigation

Observations: How will students record their observations? What information is important?

Theory: Discuss the differences in the arrangements of particles in solids, liquids and gases and ask the students to predict how this might affect sound transmission.

Supporting data: Stress that making a statement in science is similar to making a statement in history. You need evidence to support what you are saying. For example, when a student makes a statement about a historical event, they use a source to support their argument; scientists use the data to support the conclusion that they draw. Students should be encouraged to use the data in front of them to support their argument.

Answers to workbook questions

1 Students record their observations.
2 The sound travels more directly through the particles in the fingers as they are closely packed. When the fingers are out of the ears the sound then has to travel from the fingers through the air to the ear. As the particles are further apart in the air, it takes longer for the sound to reach the ear.
3 In solids the particles are packed closely together and allow the vibrations of the sound wave to transmit easily. In gases the particles are much further apart, which results in the sound taking longer to travel through the medium.
4 In the water, the particles are spaced further apart than in a solid. Whilst the sound will transmit, it will be muted compared to the sound produced when not in the water.

Answers to exam-style questions

1 A metal sheet, smooth surface such as hardwood screen. [1]
2 0.01 seconds [1]
3 speed $= \dfrac{\text{distance}}{\text{time}}$, [1] $\dfrac{800}{2.34}$, [1] 342, [1] m/s [1]
4 Repeat the experiment to achieve multiple readings [1] and find the average. [1]

Total marks [8]

13 Light

Throughout this chapter your students will be expected to
- use, or describe the use of, common techniques, apparatus and materials.
- select the most appropriate apparatus or method for a task and justify the choice made.

Practical investigation 13.1 Forming a virtual image in a mirror

Planning the investigation

During this investigation your students will:
- describe the formation of an optical image by a plane mirror, and give its characteristics
- recall that the image in a plane mirror is virtual
- perform simple constructions, measurements and calculations for reflection by plane mirrors.

This investigation can be conducted in conjunction with teaching the theory.

Duration: 30-45 minutes

Grouping: Ideally, students will work in pairs. More that two students sharing the equipment will significantly increase the time taken for the investigation, if each student is to produce an image and have experience of the practical.

Setting up for the investigation

Each pair will need: power supply, ray box, multi-slit screen, plane mirror and mount, A3 sheet of white paper, 30 cm rule

White paper is best for this exercise.

A lamp can be used instead of a ray box, if it is shielded to provide a tunnelled light source.

The power supply is not required if the ray box has an inbuilt power supply.

Equipment should be evenly distributed around the edges of the classroom to avoid crowding when students are collecting it.Students are asked to use a ray box with a multi-slit screen to form a virtual image in a plane mirror. They are expected to trace the path of the incident and reflected rays by placing crosses on the paper and using these to draw in the lines. Students are asked to use the diverging reflected rays to track back and show where the virtual image is formed in the mirror.

Key discussion points for this investigation

- **Equipment**: Why is a multi-slit screen being used? Would a single slit be appropriate? What is the precision of each of the instruments being used? How could precision be improved?
- **Accuracy**: How can the accuracy of the measurements be improved? How could the investigation be adapted to accommodate this?

- **Theory**: Why are dashed lines used to represent virtual lines? Why is the image virtual rather than real? How is the image positioned or oriented in comparison to the object? Discuss the properties of images in plane mirrors.

Safety considerations

The ray boxes can become very warm after prolonged use. Students should turn off the ray box when not in use and allow the box to cool. It should be handled with caution, to prevent burns.

Keep all electrical equipment away from water.

Make sure hands are dry before handling the electrical equipment

Common errors when conducting the investigation

Students often try to tackle all of the lines in one go, which can lead to confusion about which cross belongs to which line. Guide students into working on one set of crosses (incident and corresponding reflected ray) at a time. They can do this by colour coding the crosses or marking the crosses with a subscript number. Turning the box off and repositioning is not advised, as it can take up a lot of time and is difficult to return it to the original position.

Supporting your students

Rather than drawing the crosses, students who are struggling can look into the mirror and mark on the paper where they think the image is coming from. The practical can also be shortened by adopting this approach, if time is an issue.

Challenging your students

Students can investigate using barriers in a ripple tank to form reflections. If a variety of shapes of barrier are available, students should comment on the formation of the reflected wave fronts, for example: discussing the wavelength, velocity and frequency of the reflected waves in comparison to the incident waves.

Answers to workbook questions

1. angle of incidence = angle of reflection
2. Dashed lines represent where light appears to come from, they are virtual rays.
3. The image is the same distance from the mirror as the object is.
4. The image is:
   - the same size as the object
   - the same distance from the mirror as the object
   - upright
   - virtual.
5. A multi-slit screen shows a number of rays and the point where they converge is where the image would appear. This would not be possible using a single slit.

Practical investigation 13.2 Finding the refractive index of glass

Planning the investigation

During this investigation your students will:

- describe an experimental demonstration of the refraction of light
- recall and use the definition of refractive index n in terms of speed
- recall and use the equation $\dfrac{\sin i}{\sin r} = n$.

This investigation should be conducted after teaching the theory.

Duration: 45-60 minutes

Grouping: 2–4 students per group

Setting up for the investigation

Each group will need: semi-circular glass block, A3 sheet of white paper, power supply, single-slit screen, ray box, protractor

The semi-circular glass block should be frosted on the underside – a rectangular glass block can be used but there will be two refractions to consider, which might confuse less able students.

Students are ask to use a ray box to measure the angle of incidence and angle of refraction of a ray by directing a beam of light onto the centre of the flat side of a semi-circular glass block. The beam of light should exit through the curved side of the block. Students will then be required to plot a graph of $\sin r$ against $\sin i$ in order to calculate the refractive index of glass from the inverse of the gradient of the line of best fit.

Key discussion points for this investigation

Measurements: Where are the angles of incidence and refraction measured from? Why is a normal required? What is a normal? How can the lines be drawn accurately? What is the precision of the protractor?

Calculator: How will students calculate $\sin i$ and $\sin r$? How will students use the calculator to obtain the required readings?

Graphs: Scaling, plot, calculation of $\sin i$ and $\sin r$, how is a gradient calculated? Line of best fit: straight or curved?

Safety considerations

The ray boxes can become very warm after prolonged use. Students should turn off the ray box when not in use and allow the box to cool. It should be handled with caution to prevent burns.

Keep all electrical equipment away from water.

Make sure hands are dry before handling the electrical equipment.

Common errors when conducting the investigation

Students can be quite careless when marking the incident light and the refracted light with crosses. This causes the angles of incidence and refraction to be slightly inaccurate, which will become evident in their graph. The problem can be a good source of discussion about accuracy of measurement, before and after the investigation.

Remind students that the angles of incidence and refraction must be measured from the normal. Students often forget this, which causes errors in their results.

Supporting your students

Students who struggle to use a protractor can use a paper protractor template placed underneath the glass block. This makes it easier for the students to see the angle at which the light is travelling. Some students might require one-to-one support during this section. Students who are very capable can act as 'experts' who assist other students with reading the angles.

Challenging your students

Students who work quickly could repeat this investigation to find the refractive index of water. It is possible to use semi-circular troughs filled with water, instead of the glass blocks, to conduct the investigation. Students could also explore the optical density of a number of other materials. Perspex blocks could be used. Students should prepare a two-minute presentation on the spectroscope and how it is used in science to help determine the composition of light from other galaxies. Students can include comparisons of spectroscopic fingerprints.

1 Students should record a range of results in 5/10° intervals between 10° and 80°.

2 They calculate the sines of the angles and record them.

3 Plot a graph of sin r against sin i. The graph should be a straight line graph with gradient of approx. 1.5.

4 They draw the line of best fit.

5 Calculate the gradient of the graph using the equation provided. Gradient = 1.5

6 1 degree

7 The points should show a significant difference from the line of best fit. To ensure more accurate results, pins could be used instead of pencilled crosses, the room should be darkened.

8 If line of best fit lies in the range of the additional points, the measurements taken are accurate. If the the line of best fit falls out of these points, the results can be improved by using a sharp pencil, ensure the baseline of the protractor is lined up the normal, crosses to mark the beam of light are aligned correctly.

Practical investigation 13.3 Finding the refractive index of glass using apparent depth

Planning the investigation

During this investigation your students will:
- describe an experimental demonstration of the refraction of light
- recall and use the definition of refractive index n in terms of speed
- recall and use the equation $\frac{\sin i}{\sin r} = n$

This investigation should be conducted after teaching the theory.

Duration: 30-40 minutes

Grouping: 2–4 students per group

Setting up for the investigation

Students are asked to find the image of an upright optical pin formed in the glass block. They are then expected to measure the real and apparent depth and calculate an average. From this data students will calculate the refractive index of the glass block.

Key discussion points for this investigation

- **Theory**: What is the refractive index? How would the refractive index be affected if the dimensions of the block were to change or the glass was to be heated? What does 'parallax mean'? Parallax is the apparent difference in position of an object when it is viewed from different positions. To have 'no parallax' between two objects, when viewed, the objects should be directly in line with one another.

Safety considerations

Ensure the floor is clear of pins to avoid injury to feet during the investigation.

Pins should be firmly secured into the cork surface to prevent injury.

Common errors when conducting the investigation

Students might struggle to understand the term 'no parallax'. They need to align their second pin so that it is completely in line with the image formed by the optical pin. Cork boards should be placed underneath the glass block to stop pins from falling or tilting while students are trying to position the second pin on the block.

Supporting your students

Set up the practical on the front bench. This allows students to see how the investigation should look and also gives a visual, to describe the meaning of the term parallax.

Challenging your students

Students should create a booklet aimed at students in lower grades (11–14 year-olds), that covers the physics behind real and apparent depth. They should include real-life examples such as a brick in the water in a swimming pool and a straw in a glass
Half fill a beaker with water. Underneath the beaker place a coin with a small amount of water on top. The coin should disappear. Ask students to research why this happens and report their results to the rest of the group.

Answers to workbook questions

1 The students record their results in the table.
2 The students calculate and record the average real depth.
3 The students calculate and record the average apparent depth.
4 The students calculate and record the average value of $\dfrac{\text{real depth}}{\text{apparent depth}}$ in the range of 1.45 – 1.51.
5 The students state the value of the refractive index of the glass block based on their answer to Q4.
6 The students compare the actual value to their calculated values. The calculated value is similar to the accepted value of 1.5. This shows that the measurements that were taken were accurate. The results are not similar. It was difficult to align the pins, the pins kept moving, making it difficult to measure the real and apparent depth.
7 The student might have misaligned the image and the pin, the second pin might have moved position, might have measured the distances incorrectly.
8 The student could use sticky tac to keep the second pin in place, use a marker to mark where the second pin is positioned, or any sensible suggestion.

Practical investigation 13.4 Estimating the magnification of a magnifying glass

Planning the investigation

During this investigation your students will:
- use and describe the use of a single lens as a magnifying glass
- show understanding of the terms real image and virtual image

This investigation can be taught in conjunction with the theory.

Duration: 25 minutes

Grouping: 2–3 students per group is ideal for this investigation.

Setting up for the investigation

Each group will need: metre rule, sticky tac, plano-convex lens +14D, screen with graph paper stuck on it, a 2 cm by 5 cm strip of card (the object), lamp, clamp stand, clamp and boss

Purpose built mounts for the metre rule can be purchased that give slightly better results for this investigation.

Equipment should be evenly distributed around the room, with the lenses positioned on the front bench so they can be handed out and counted back in easily. Students are asked to use a magnifying glass to observe the image of a given object. They will need to align the image on a screen whilst looking through a magnifying glass. From this image they should be able to estimate a magnification.

Key discussion points for this investigation

- **Accuracy in method**: How can accurate results be ensured – darken the room, use a set square to ensure all equipment is at right angles to the surface; use a scale on the screen; object and lens must be at the same height (parallax error); move the screen rather than the object.
- **Equipment**: Ask students to justify why they are using each piece of equipment and suggest alternatives that are inappropriate to stimulate students into thinking about the choice of apparatus.

Safety considerations

The lamp can become very warm after prolonged use. Students should turn off the lamp when not in use and allow it to cool before handling.

Keep all electrical equipment away from water.

Make sure hands are dry before handling the electrical equipment.

Common errors when conducting the investigation

Students will commonly struggle to form the image on the screen correctly (see below).

Supporting your students

Students might find it difficult to focus the image on the screen or be sure about how to obtain the image. Set up a station of equipment on the front bench that has already been calibrated so that students can come and see how the image might be formed. Results can be used from this equipment if students continue to struggle.

Challenging your students

Students could choose to research one of the following telescopes: James Webb, Herschel, Hubble, Spitzer space telescope. Students should produce an A4 poster on how the telescopes are constructed, what they are hoping to observe and how they manage to magnify the images they are recording.

Answers to workbook questions

1   The students record their height measurements.
2   The students calculate the magnification of the lens.
3   Work in a darkened room; use a set square to ensure all equipment is at right angles to the bench; ensure the object is at the same height as the lens.
4   To measure the height of the image accurately.

Answers to exam-style questions

1   1 cm [1]
2   3 cm [1]
3   3 [1]
4   4 cm [1]
5   11.6 cm [1]
6   2.9 [1]
7   Yes and a suitable reason given with reference to results. [2]
8   Lens at the same height as object; in a dark room; all equipment at right angles to the bench; ruler fixed to the bench. [2]

Total marks [10]

14 Properties of waves

This chapter contains investigations on:

◆ **3.1** General wave properties

Throughout this chapter your students will be expected to:
- make and record observations, measurements and estimates
- interpret and evaluate experimental observations.

Practical investigation 14.1 Waves on a spring

Planning the investigation

During this investigation your students will:
- demonstrate understanding that waves transfer energy without transferring matter
- describe what is meant by wave motion, as illustrated by vibration in springs
- give the meaning of speed, frequency, wavelength and amplitude
- distinguish between transverse and longitudinal waves and give suitable examples.

This investigation can be done in conjunction with teaching the theory.

Duration: 20 minutes

Grouping: ideally 3 per group, depending on availability of equipment and class size

Setting up for the investigation

Each group will need: large spring, metre rule, stopwatch
The equipment can be placed at the ends of the front bench and the students can collect what they need from either side. In this practical, students are asked to create both transverse and longitudinal waves on the spring and measure the speed of each wave they create

Safety considerations

Students should take care with the spring in case it springs back and causes injury. They should also handle the spring with care, to prevent injury when sending wave fronts down the spring.

Common errors when conducting the investigation

When calculating the speed of the wave, students might forget that the distance travelled is **double** the length of the spring. This should be highlighted before calculations are completed.

Supporting your students

Students might find the calculation the most challenging part. Work this through as a class discussion. Leaving an example on the board for reference may help.

Challenging your students

Students could research the types of wave involved in earthquakes. They can write an information leaflet about how they are formed, transmitted through the ground and how to stay safe during an earthquake. Students could research tsunami waves. How and why are they formed? Students can prepare a two-minute presentation on how tsunami waves are created and why they cause so much damage, giving examples of some of the most recent tsunami events.
Polarisation is a behaviour exhibited only by transverse waves. Students could research how waves are polarised and give examples of what polarisation is used for.

Key discussion points for the investigation

- **Key features of waves**: These are wavelength, frequency, velocity, crests, troughs, compressions, rarefaction. Discussion should also focus around reflection of a wave from a fixed point and how this occurs for all types of waves. How does changing the speed affect the wavelength or the frequency? Why is important to be able to identify waves based on their properties? For example, UV, X-rays and gamma radiation can all cause damage to human cells due to their high frequency.

- **Importance of waves**: Waves carry energy from one place to another without transferring matter. Some waves can travel through a vacuum, for example, electromagnetic waves travel through space. Why is this important? Without their ability to transfer this energy, we would not receive the Sun's thermal energy and life would cease to exist, as Earth would be too cold. Without light from the Sun, nothing would grow. Communications are dependent on waves, smart phones for example, only work because of the ability of waves to transfer energy.

- **Method**: How can students calculate the speed of a wave? What equation will they use? What measurements will they take? How are they going to record the time it takes for the wave to travel from a fixed point and back again? Use video on tablets or phones with timing and freeze-framing capability, or stopwatches. What will the distance be if it is a reflected wave?

- **Drawing diagrams of waves on springs**: How are the spring curves drawn? Where are labels placed? Labelling of diagrams – where are the peaks, troughs, wavelengths on each of the waveforms?

Answers to workbook questions

1   The students record their results in the table.
2   The students sketch a transverse wave, labelling the amplitude.
3   As the speed of the wave is increased the frequency also increases. The wavelength might also shorten.
4   The students sketch a longitudinal wave, labelling a compression and a rarefaction.
5   **Difficulty**: Timing the wavefront.
    Solution: Record, using video and stop frame for exact time.
    Or:
    Difficulty: Maintaining a fixed end. **Solution**: Fix to a wall rather than use another person.

Practical investigation 14.2
Investigating the properties of waves

Planning the investigation

During this investigation your students will:
- describe how waves can undergo:
  - ○ reflection at a plane surface
  - ○ refraction due to a change of speed
  - ○ diffraction through a narrow gap
- describe the use of water waves to demonstrate reflection, refraction and diffraction
- describe how wavelength and gap size affects diffraction through a gap
- describe how wavelength affects diffraction at an edge.

This demonstration should be conducted as a complement to teaching the theory.

Duration: 45 minutes including drawing wave front diagrams

Grouping: Students work individually or in pairs

Setting up for the investigation

This activity can be broken into three smaller demonstrations, as introductory pieces for other sections on waves.

In addition to a ripple tank, they will need a straight barrier (reflection), a trapezoid of plastic (refraction), two straight barriers (diffraction). During this demonstration students are asked to describe how the waves are established and to record any observations they have made about the properties of waves.

Safety considerations

HH

Take care with students suffering from epilepsy or who have seizures triggered by flashing lights.

Ensure the placement of the ripple tank is away from plug sockets due to potential exposure to water.

Common errors when conducting the investigation

Refraction

The water on top of the trapezoid needs to be extremely shallow. Fill the top tray with water until the plastic is well covered, then slowly drain out the water so that only the smallest amount of water remains. This should make

refraction of the wave much more visible for the students. Use a low frequency on the dipper to demonstrate.

Diffraction

Keep the frequency of the motor low to get good results from this experiment otherwise vibrations might cause the barriers also to vibrate and give false results.

Supporting your students

Students tend to struggle with **why** refraction occurs. To demonstrate refraction, select six students and ask them to link arms tightly to form a 'wave front'. On the floor, draw a chalk line representing the boundary between two media. Direct the 'wave front' towards the boundary, inclined at approximately 45°. Students should walk at the same pace to the boundary and as soon as each student 'hits' the boundary they should walk in smaller steps. This causes the wave front to bend, demonstrating to students that the change in speed is what causes the refraction.

Challenging your students

Students can investigate whether circular ripples behave in the same way as straight parallel waves. They can to use the ripple tank (under supervision from a technician if the teacher is not available) to generate circular ripples, to investigate how they behave through a narrow gap, a large gap and a single barrier. They should note down any observations made.

Key discussion points for this investigation

- **Demo setup**: Explain how the ripple tank works. Talk through the frequency at which the bar oscillates, how the bar strikes the water to create vibrations that are seen as wave fronts. Explain the equipment you are using to act as boundaries and the impact they are having in the water.
- **Reflection**: Start with the wave front hitting the boundary along the normal. Start to change the angle of the boundary and ask students to observe what is happening with the angle of reflection, the wavelength, the speed and frequency of the waves.
- **Refraction**: Show students that the water above the boundary is shallower and explain the reasoning behind why the water slows down in shallower water (due to increased friction with the seabed). If the wave

speed is reduced, what might the impact be on the wavelength and frequency? Why does the direction change as it enters shallower waters? Why might the direction change as it gets into deeper water?

● **Diffraction:** Start by showing how diffraction occurs at a corner so only put one barrier in place. Students can also sketch this if they wish. Place the second barrier. Discuss with students the wavelength in comparison to the gap size. Guide them into making the correlation between the amount of diffraction and the size of the gap in comparison to wavelength.

1   The students sketch the reflection of a wavefront from the boundary, using straight lines to represent the waveform.
2   The wavelength and the speed remain constant.
3   The angle of the incoming wave front is equal to the angle of the reflected wave front.
4   The shallow water boundary causes the speed of the wavefront to decrease. This slowing of the wavefront causes the wave front to bend.
5   The wave speed decreases as it enters the more shallow water. The frequency of the wavefront remains constant so the wavelength must also decrease.
6   The students draw a diagram of the wave front before and after it hits the boundary in the water.

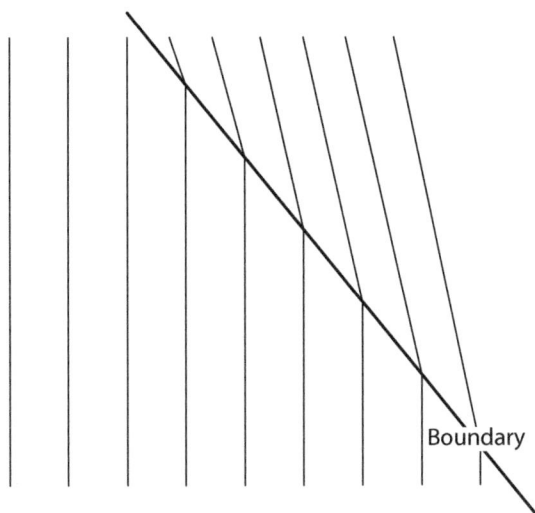

Boundary

7   Students draw a diagram of waves passing through a large gap and a small gap. They describe the wave pattern, speed and wavelength after the wave passes through the gap. See CD-ROM for an example.

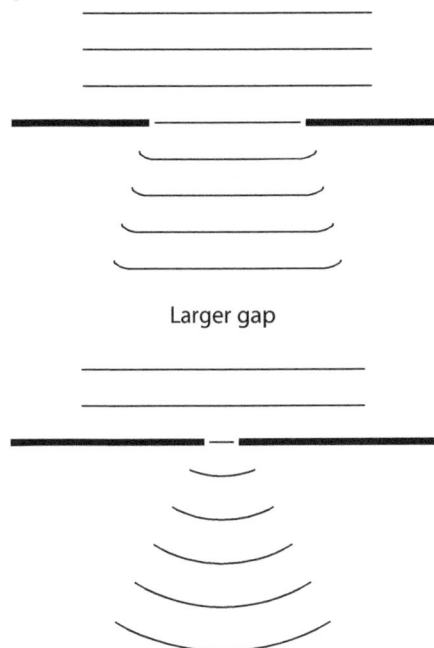

Larger gap

8   Waves are generated by a beam attached to a motor. The motor oscillates the beam, disrupting the surface of the water producing waves.
9   As the wave front travels into shallower water the wave slows down, and consequently changes its direction.
10   The closer the gap in size to the wavelength of the wave, the greater the diffraction that occurs.
11   The wavelength of light is much smaller than the wavelength of the water waves. This means a much smaller gap in the order of 10^{-7} m would need to be used in order to see the diffraction of the light.

1 Transverse wave [1]

2 Any four from: Place bar in the water, set motor running, measure the size of gap, record observations; repeat for different sizes of gap. [4]

3

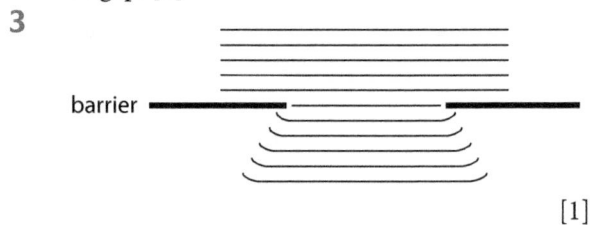

[1]

wavelength remains the same; [1]
small diffraction [1]

4

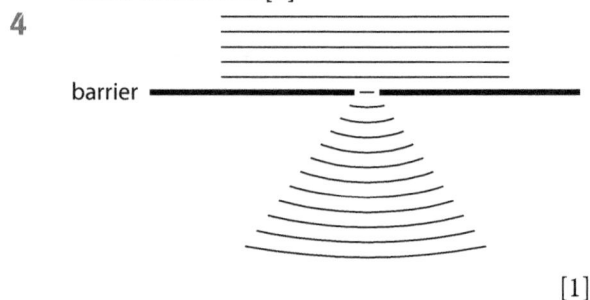

[1]

wavelength remains the same; [1]
large diffraction [1]

5 The closer the gap to the size of the wavelength, [1] the greater the diffraction observed. [1]

6 Observe in a darkened room; ensure the beam is submerged in the water; ensure the frequency of the waves is low. [1]

Total marks [14]

15 Spectra

Throughout this chapter your students will be expected to:
- use, or describe the use of, common techniques, apparatus and materials, for example, ray-tracing
- make estimates or describe outcomes that demonstrate their familiarity with an experiment, procedure or technique
- select the most appropriate apparatus or method for a task and justify the choice made.

Practical investigation 15.1 Dispersion of white light

Planning the investigation

During this investigation your students should be aiming towards:
- giving a qualitative account of the dispersion of light, as shown by the action on light of a glass prism and including listing the seven colours of the spectrum in their correct order.

This investigation can be taught in conjunction with the theory.

Duration: 20 minutes

Grouping: Ideally 2 per group, with a maximum of 4 to a group depending on the equipment available.

Setting up for the investigation

Each group will need: a power supply, ray box, single-slit slide, A3 sheet of white paper, 60° prism, white screen and stand

Equipment should be evenly distributed around the edges of the classroom to avoid crowding when students are collecting it.

Keep prisms on the front bench so they can easily be counted out and in. In this investigation students will set up a ray box and prism, to split white light into its constituent parts. Students will be expected to draw a diagram of the spectra that they find and will be asked to explain how it forms.

Safety considerations

The ray boxes can become very warm after prolonged use. Students should turn off the ray box when it is not in use and allow the box to cool and handle with caution to prevent burns.

Common errors when conducting the investigation

It can be difficult to get the spectrum clearly visible at first. Students need to be patient and keep trying. They should ensure they are aiming the single slit towards the middle of one of the sides of the prism. If students still struggle, the beam can be passed through a cylindrical lens (+7D) before the prism to sharpen the image.

Supporting your students

Demonstrate refraction. Select six students and ask them to link arms tightly to form a 'wave front'. On the floor, draw a chalk line representing the boundary between two media. Direct the 'wave front' towards the boundary, inclined at approximately 45°. Students should walk at the same pace to the boundary.

As soon as a student 'hits' the boundary, they should walk in smaller steps. This causes the wave front to bend, demonstrating to students that the change in speed is what causes the refraction.

Challenging your students

Students should investigate the impact of coloured filters on the light before it passes into the prism and after it passes out of the prism. They can predict what they think might happen and then record their observations, giving reasons for why they think this is occurring.

Students should produce an informative poster on the formation of rainbows.

Key points for discussion in this investigation

- **Equipment**: A single-slit slide is chosen so that interference between two slits does not occur and a clear basic spectrum is formed. Students could suggest reasons for using a single slit or a clear glass prism. Would it be beneficial to use a lens? If so why?
- **Theory**: Why does the white light split? Why do the different colours appear separately in a specific order? Why are some refracted more than others? How could the white light be recombined? Why would using a second prism cause the light to recombine?
- **Reliability**: How can students ensure the spectrum they see is reliable? Use a darkened room, ensure they are using a white light source, use a single-slit slide, or other sensible suggestions.
- **Further discussion**: This could be related to the use of filters. If a coloured filter was placed before the prism, what might we expect to see? If the filter is placed after the prism would the same effect be visible? What might we expect to see?

Answers to workbook questions

1 As the prism is rotated the width of the spectrum of the refracted beam gets smaller and then larger as the rotation continues.

2 Students should sketch and label the colours in order: red, orange, yellow, green, blue, indigo, violet.

3 Red, orange, yellow, green, blue, indigo, violet.

4 Violet. The glass slows down the violet light more than it does the red and so the angle through which the violet is refracted is greater.

5 View the spectrum in a darkened room, use a white screen, use a lens to sharpen the image.

6 Interference from the multiple-slit sources will produce a different pattern to the basic spectrum.

7 A beam of white light is observed. The incident light on the second prism changes speed as it enters the glass block. This causes the spectrum to be refracted by different amounts, dependent on their wavelengths, back into the original beam of white light.

Practical investigation 15.2 Investigating infrared waves

Planning the investigation

During this investigation your students will:

- describe the main features of the electromagnetic spectrum in order of wavelength
- describe typical properties and uses of radiations in all the different regions of the electromagnetic spectrum, including:
  - ○ radio and television communications (radio waves)
  - ○ satellite television and telephones (microwaves)
  - ○ electrical appliances, remote controllers for televisions and intruder alarms (infrared).

This can be taught in conjunction with the theory.

Duration: 30 minutes

Grouping: 2–4 students per group, depending on the availability of equipment.

Setting up for the investigation

Each group will need: infrared source, infrared thermometer, testing materials, clamp stand, clamp and boss, metre rule

The materials they are testing should include sheets of cardboard, aluminium foil, a metal grille, a cardboard box and plastic sheets.

This investigation can be conducted with microwaves and radiowaves, dependent on the availability of transmitters and receivers.

Depending on the number of students and availability of equipment, this can be run as a station-based activity. In this investigation, students are asked to devise an investigation to test what materials block the transmission of infrared radiation.

Safety considerations

MH

Students must not aim the infrared source directly towards another student.

Supporting your students

Give students an exemplar method to follow, that requires them to fill in the extra details such as variables and table of results.

Challenging your students

Options to extend some of the investigations include conducting the investigation for other forms of radiation such as radiowaves and microwaves.

Radiowaves: Investigate if the aluminium foil bocks all frequencies of radiowaves.

Microwaves: Research how microwave ovens work and prepare an information poster.

Infrared: Investigate how temperature decreases with distance from the object.

Key discussion points for this investigation

- **Variables**: Independent variables – type of blocking material; dependent variables – intensity of radiation; control variables – distance from transmitter, positioning of material (for example, as a sheet or wrapped around something else), thickness of material where possible.
- **Method**: How will students conduct the investigation? Where will they position the materials? How will they record a change in intensity? Infrared thermometer, microwave receiver, by ear for the radio.
- **Control variables**: How will students adapt their investigation to ensure that they are indeed controlled in their investigation? What will students control and how will they do it?

Answers to workbook questions

1 Students draw a table for their results.

Material	Intensity /W/m²			
	1	2	3	Average

2 Aluminium foil blocked the greatest amount of radiation. This can be seen in the results as the reading on the infrared thermometer dropped to 8 W/m².

3

Variable	Control
thickness of material	all the same thickness where possible – 1 layer
distance from transmitter	same distance each time
positioning of material	same size squares each time

Answers to exam-style questions

1 Independent: type of sunscreen [1]
Dependent: amount of fluorescence [1]
2 Two from: the distance of acetate from the UV light, [1] the volume of sunscreen, coverage of acetate, [1] same UV light, [1] same volume of fluorescent matter. [1]
3 The acetate is transparent and will not block any of the UV light. [1]
4 Ensure all variables that might affect the results are controlled and repeat the experiment to see if the results are the same. [1]

Total marks [6]

16 Magnetism

This chapter contains investigations on:

◆ **4.1** Simple phenomena of magnetism

Throughout this chapter your students will be expected to:
- identify key variables and describe how, or explain why, certain variables should be controlled
- draw an appropriate conclusion, justifying it by reference to the data and using an appropriate explanation
- comment critically on a procedure or point of practical detail and suggest an appropriate improvement.

Practical investigation 16.1 A magnetic circus

Planning the investigation

During this investigation your students will:
- distinguish between magnetic and non-magnetic materials
- draw the pattern of magnetic field lines around a bar magnet
- describe an experiment to identify the pattern of magnetic field lines, including the direction.

This experiment can be conducted in conjunction with the theory.

Duration: 30 minutes

Grouping: 2–4 students per group, depending on class size and availability of equipment.

Setting up for the investigation

Equipment
Station 1: two magnets with ends marked N and S
Station 2: magnet, copper strips, iron nails, steel ball bearings, nickel strips, wooden pegs, aluminium strips

Station 3: magnets, plastic film, an A3 sheet of white paper, iron filings

Students may be given any combinations of materials, magnetic and non-magnetic.

For station 3, magnets can be wrapped in plastic film to prevent iron filings from touching them directly.

Set up the equipment in at least six stations, depending on class size and equipment availability, before the beginning of the lesson. Students are asked to conduct four small investigations. In the first they bring two magnets together to determine the relationship between same poles and opposite poles. In the second, they determine which materials are magnetic and which are not. In the third experiment, students use iron filings to detect magnetic field lines. Each of these experiments can be extended out to a stand-alone activity for which students design their own method.

Safety considerations

Students should avoid touching their faces and wash their hands at the end of the session to prevent iron filings from getting into their eyes

Common errors when conducting the investigation

Station 1: Students might not know which pole is which, if they are using plastic-coated magnets and the magnet inside has been switched over. Check magnets before the session to ensure that the polarity is correctly marked.
Station 2: Steel is magnetic, but the strength depends on the iron content within the steel. It is worth clarifying with the students that it is the iron within the steel that is responding to the magnet.

Station 3: For a distinct field line pattern to be observed, students should use the iron filings generously. Students should ensure the filings do not come into contact with the magnet as they will be very difficult to remove.

Supporting your students

It is possible to buy or make – before the session – the field patterns of interacting magnetic fields. The paper can be laminated to hold the iron filings in place. Students can work directly from these or from researched pictures on the internet if they have access.

Challenging your students

Students can be given a small ring of ferrite that has been pre-magnetised. Ask students to predict how the field lines will form around this ferrite ring. They can then manipulate the rings and use iron filings to test if they are indeed magnetic. Place the rings in plastic film if using iron filings, so the filings can be easily removed. Students can break the ferrite rings if they wish. This should expose the fact that the magnetic field runs in a circular pattern throughout the ring.

Key discussion points for this investigation

- **Accuracy:** How can students obtain more accurate results? How could they adapt the methods to incorporate this?
- **Methods:** Why has plastic film been used around the magnets? How could students remove the iron fillings without using this?
- **Variables:** What other variables are there to consider in the experiments?
- **Magnetic material:** Discuss distance from the magnet, composition of the material, whether it is coated?
- **Drawing conclusions:** Students use their results to support any statements made. Draw on experience with other subjects that use sources to support their arguments. The approach in science is similar.

Answers to workbook questions

1   The north pole of a bar magnet will attract the south pole of another magnet. The magnetic field lines run from the north pole to the south which causes the opposing ends to move towards one another. When like poles are placed opposite one another the force felt from the field lines causes a repulsion.

2   Students comment on the results of their investigation at Station 2 and their prediction.

3   The field lines run in a circular pattern on the outside of the bar magnet, running from one pole to the other. The iron filings cluster at the poles, suggesting these are the strongest points of the magnet.

4   The magnetic materials were those that were attracted by the magnet. These materials included nickel and iron.

5   Unlike poles attract each other, whereas like poles repel each other.

6   Secure the paper to two supporting rings acting like a bridge over the magnet.
    The magnet can be repositioned by moving the paper.

7   For the materials identified as possibly magnetic, the opposite side of the magnet should be used to see if the material still attracts. If it is a magnet it would be repelled by the test magnet.

Practical investigation 16.2
Exploring magnetic fields

Planning the investigation

During this investigation your students will:
- draw the pattern of magnetic field lines around a bar magnet
- describe an experiment to identify the pattern of magnetic field lines, including the direction.

This practical can be taught in conjunction with the theory.

Duration: 20 minutes
Grouping: Maximum of 3 per group.

Setting up for the investigation

Each group will need: 3 magnets (one for the extension), white paper, plotting compass
The equipment can be evenly distributed around the room so that no clustering occurs. Students are asked to investigate the field line patterns produced when two magnetic fields interact. They will be required to use plotting compasses and white paper.

Key discussion points for this investigation

- **Method**: How can the method be adapted to make it easier to see the field pattern? For example: use card rather than paper, supports under the card to act like a bridge so the magnet can be manipulated without moving the card. How else could this investigation be performed? Ask students to predict which way the field lines will connect based on their previous knowledge.
- **Sketching**: what is important to include in a sketch? Does it need to be labelled?

Safety considerations

Plotting compasses should be stored correctly to ensure demagnetisation does not occur.

Common errors when conducting the investigation

Students can sometimes put the wrong poles together, so the results display the wrong pattern. Some magnets with outer blue and red plastic casings might display the wrong results, which can be confusing. This is a result of the magnet being inverted inside the casing. It is worth checking before and after each session that the magnets are correctly positioned inside the casing and that uncased magnets have correctly labelled poles.

Supporting your students

It is possible to buy or make laminated field patterns from iron filings. Images of field patterns can also be downloaded from the internet. Students can use these for guidance about what to expect when using plotting compasses.

Challenging your students

Field lines are not just two-dimensional. Ask students to use modelling clay to predict what the field lines around a bar magnet might look like in 3D. They can use a bar magnet at the centre.

Answers to workbook questions

1   Students sketch the results for opposite poles facing: N–S.

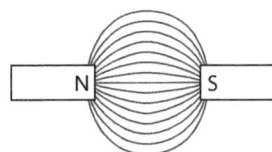

attraction

2   Students sketch the results for same poles facing: N–N, S–S.

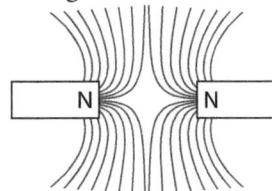

repulsion

3   The field lines from the north pole of one magnet connect to the south pole of the other magnet. The outer field lines still curve but the inner ones are closely packed together. Field lines around each magnet still connect from north to south.

4   The field lines are closest together near the poles so the field is strongest here.
Iron filings can be used to display the magnetic fields.

5 The field lines for three magnets will look like this.

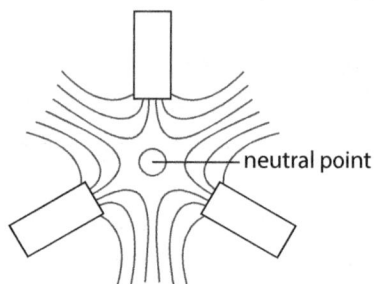

neutral point

6 Iron filings or steel pins.

Practical investigation 16.3
Investigating electromagnets

Planning the investigation

During this investigation your students will:
- distinguish between the magnetic properties of soft iron and steel
- distinguish between the design and use of permanent magnets and electromagnets.

This investigation should be conducted in conjunction with the theory.

Duration: 45–60 minutes including extension. Approximately 15 minutes per section.

Grouping: This will depend on number of stations but ideally students should work in groups of 2–3, so that they can all experience manipulating equipment.

Setting up for the investigation

Each station should have a locked power pack, a long coil of insulated copper wire and several paperclips. Using a longer length of copper wire will mean that the number of coils can be varied.

This investigation can be adapted so that students set up the equipment, if the time is available, or it is set up beforehand if time is restricted. Ideally, set up a minimum of eight stations: four for each investigation. Additional extension stations could be set up, each with a soft iron core, an ammeter set up in the circuit and a variable resistor. There are two stations in this investigation and students will be asked to investigate the effect of the type of core and number of turns on the coil on the strength of an electromagnet.

Safety considerations

This investigation will require trialling before running, to ascertain safe working limits of current for the equipment being used so no overheating of the wire occurs. Students should turn off the power pack when the electromagnet is not in use, to prevent risk of burns from overheating.

Common errors when conducting the investigation

When students try to load paperclips onto the electromagnet, some might be in chains, linked to each other, which can skew the results. Discuss this at the beginning of the investigation and encourage students to decide on a best method for loading the paperclips. If possible, lock power packs at a set p.d. so that the students do not consider this as a variable. If the power pack is not locked students sometimes try to manipulate two variables at once.

Supporting your students

Students can struggle with the concept that the bar's magnetism can be turned on and off. Demonstrate this, with students being the domains within a demagnetised iron bar. Place a sticky note with an arrow on each student. Face students in different directions. Explain that when the current passes down the wire surrounding the iron bar this causes all the domains to align in the same direction, which creates the magnetic field around the bar. When the coil is turned off, the domains go back to their original positions and thus the bar is demagnetised.

Challenging your students

A third station could be set up in advance for this investigation.
Station 3: Soft iron core, ammeter set up in circuit, variable resistor, insulated copper wire
Students can design and conduct an investigation into the impact of current on the strength of an electromagnet. In their method they should include:
- the independent, dependent and control variables in their investigation
- how to conduct the practical
- the measurements they will take
- how they will make sure they have accurate results.

Key discussion points for this investigation

- **Variables**: Discuss control variables for each element of the investigation and reasoning for why they need to be controlled.
- **Accuracy**: Picking up paperclips can be inaccurate. How will students ensure accuracy in their measurement? Will they add paperclips one at a time, or will they just stroke the rod over the pile of paperclips and see how many it picks up?

- **Conclusions**: How can students use the data to support their conclusion? Ask students, in groups, to write what they think a poor, mid-range and excellent answer would look like. As a class, create an excellent answer.

Answers to workbook questions

Station 1
1 The independent variable is the type of core, the dependent variable is the strength of the electromagnet, the control variables are p.d. supplied (effectively the current supplied), the number of turns, type of paperclips each time.
2 Wrap the insulated copper wire around the steel core 40 times.
Attach either end of the insulated copper wire to the crocodile clips, which are connected to the power supply.
Turn on the power supply.
Place the steel core over the paperclips and record how many are picked up by the core.
Repeat the above steps for the other two types of core.
3 The students prepare a table for results.

Type of core	Number of paperclips picked up		
	1	2	Average

4 The core made from soft iron was the most effective in the electromagnet. The soft iron core picked up 28 paperclips compared to just 1 paperclip in the steel. The wooden core did not magnetise as it failed to pick up any paperclips. The number of coils and the current were kept constant so as not to impact upon the results.

Station 2
1 The independent variable is the number of turns, the dependent variable is the strength of the electromagnet, the control variables are the type of core, the p.d. supplied (effectively the current supplied).

2 Wrap the insulated copper wire around the steel core 20 times.

Attach either end of the insulated copper wire to the crocodile clips which are connected to the main supply.

Turn on the power supply.

Place the steel core over the paperclips and record how many are picked up by the core.

Repeat for increasing number of turns in the wire.

3 The students prepare a table for results.

Number of turns	Number of paperclips		
	1	2	Average
20			
40			
60			
80			
100			

4 As the number of turns on the coil of wire was increased, the number of paperclips collected by the electromagnet also increased. For example, when there were 20 turns only 15 paperclips were collected compared to when there were 80 turns and 48 paperclips were picked up. The core and current were kept constant so as not to impact upon the results.

Questions

1 The potential difference was kept at the same value throughout the experiment to ensure the current within the circuit remained constant. The number of turns on the coil was kept at 40 so that this did not affect the result.

2 A steel core would not demagnetise. Altering the core would impact upon the strength of the magnet.

3 Any reasonable suggestion such as: loaded one paper clip at a time; made sure no paperclips were linked; only added the paperclips in a chain.

4 To ensure reliable results and disregard any anomalous results.

Answers to exam-style questions

1 Increase the number of turns on the coil or use a soft iron core. [1]

2 The iron nail, [1] as it can become magnetised. [1]

3 Plastic is not a magnetic material. [1]

4 The number of turns on the coil. [1]

5 9 [1]

6 Any sensible suggestion: miscounted paperclips; there might have been a break in the circuit and the bar still had some remaining magnetism. [2]

7 As the current through the wire increases the strength of the bar magnet also increases. [1] When the current was 0.2 A it could hold 4 paperclips but as the current increased to 1.0 A it increased to 36 paperclips. [1]

Total marks [10]

17 Static electricity

Throughout this chapter your students will be expected to:
- make estimates or describe outcomes which demonstrate their familiarity with an experiment, procedure or technique
- draw an appropriate conclusion, justifying it by reference to the data and using an appropriate explanation
- plan an experiment or investigation including making reasoned predictions of expected results and suggesting suitable apparatus and techniques.

Practical investigation 17.1 Investigating static electricity

Planning the investigation

During this investigation your students will:
- state that there are positive and negative charges
- state that unlike charges attract and that like charges repel
- describe simple experiments to show the production and detection of electrostatic charges.

This practical can be taught in conjunction with the theory.

Duration: 35 minutes

Grouping: Ideally, students work in groups of 3.

Setting up for the investigation

Equipment

Station 1: 2 polythene rods, 2 acrylic rods, woollen cloth, watch glass

Station 2: salt, pencil shavings, woollen cloths, sheet of paper, balloon

Any finely ground table salt should work or rock salt to make the separation easier to view.

Station 3: 2 balloons, string, piece of cloth, water bottle with sprayer

Any latex style balloons may be used, but check for latex allergies before the lesson. Students should be able to blow up the balloons, although this can be done before the lesson if time is short. Students with a latex allergy can use two polystyrene balls attached to string instead. Set up the equipment in stations around the room. There should be at least nine stations (three of each), dependent on group size and availability of equipment. The students will carry out three activities.

Station 1: Investigate how charges on acrylic and polythene rods interact with each other.

Station 2: Try to separate salt from pencil shavings by using a charged balloon.

Station 3: Investigate how the charges on two balloons interact in dry air and wet air.

Safety considerations

HH

Before the lesson, check whether students have latex allergies. Any student with such an allergy should use polystyrene balls suspended on string.

Before the lesson, check whether any students have a pacemaker fitted. Take care in case, when charging up objects, these students are not also charging themselves.

Clean up water spillages on the floor immediately, to prevent slippages.

Common errors when conducting the investigation

- **Station 1**: If a charged rod is over handled it can become discharged. Encourage students to handle the rods as little as possible once they have been charged.
- **Station 2**: If this investigation is done on paper, it can give a confusing result. If the balloon is brought too near the paper, both the salt and the pencil shavings will be attracted to the balloon. To reduce the likelihood of this happening, place the salt and pencil shavings on the woollen cloth rather than the plate. This will retain more of the salt as the induced charge on the cloth will attract the salt.
- **Station 3**: If the charged balloon is over-handled it can become discharged, as the student will earth the excess charge. Once a balloon has been rubbed, students should use the string to manipulate it. If their results seem incorrect students can mark a spot X on each balloon and only rub this section, so they know which part of the balloon they have charged. They can then bring the two sections marked X together to see what happens.

Supporting your students

This can be modelled with students. Students generally confuse which particles are moving where and why. Select student to mimic the particles in a cloth and an acrylic rod. Give students sticky notes bearing a + or a -. Rub the two groups of students together (mimicking friction between the two) and remove some electrons from one material to the other. Ask the weaker students to identify the charges now remaining on the cloth and the rod and ask them to assess the overall charge on each.

Challenging your students

Students should research electrostatics in action in items such as a printer, paint sprayer and electrostatic precipitator. Students should construct a presentation that explains in basic terms how one of these works and explain it to the group.

Key discussion points for this investigation

- **Method**: How will students charge insulators/ isolated conductors? Why should they reduce handling once the materials are charged? Why would a woollen cloth provide a charge through

friction? What other practicals can they think of, that involved statics?
- **Results**: How will students record observations? Are results always best tabulated? What other ways can they be documented?
- **Theory**: What do the results imply? How can this be used to write a conclusion?

Answers to workbook questions

Station 1

As the two rods are brought together they move towards one another. They attract. This suggests that the two rods have opposite charges. When two rods of the same material are brought towards one another, the rods move away from one another, they repel. This suggests they have similar charges.

Station 2

As the balloon is brought over the salt and pencil shavings it attracts them. As the pencil shavings are lighter they stick to the balloon more quickly. Both the salt and the pencil shavings have an opposite charge to the balloon and so are attracted to it. The charge in the shavings is induced due to the charge on the balloon. The pencil shavings, being lighter, are easier to lift.

Station 3

Balloon condition	Observations
uncharged balloons	lie side by side
charged balloons	balloons separate
dampened balloons	balloons almost return to rest position

Both of the balloons obtain the same charge because they are made of the same material and so they repel one another.

The water conducts electrons and so conducts the static charge away so that the balloons are no longer charged.

Questions

1   The like charges repel, the unlike charges attract
2   Reduced handling of items that have been charged.
3   Earth themselves by touching a conductor; remove rubber-soled shoes.

Practical investigation 17.2
Charging by induction

Planning the investigation

During this investigation your students will:
- give an account of charging by induction
- describe simple experiments to show the production and detection of electrostatic charges
- distinguish between electrical conductors and insulators and give typical examples.

This investigation should be conducted in conjunction with the theory.

Duration: 60 minutes including design and practical

Grouping: Ideally, groups of 4 to allow for collaboration.

Setting up for the investigation

Each group will need: balloons, woollen cloth, concrete wall, wood, glass, small pieces of paper, pencil shavings

The classroom wall should be suitable for this activity. Any strip of wood or wooden surface may be used. For safety, windows are preferable to sheets of glass. Small pieces of waste paper can be used.

Students can sharpen a pencil to make the shavings. Space the equipment evenly around the outside of the room to prevent crowding.

Students are asked to devise an investigation to find out which materials can be charged by induction from a charged balloon. This will be evident because the balloon will stick to the material.

Charging by induction can also be demonstrated using an gold leaf electroscope and Perspex rod.

Safety considerations

HH

Wooden planks should be handled with caution in case they cause injury.

Students should take care when touching their faces during the practical and wash their hands at the end to ensure that no pencil shavings reach their eyes.

Common errors when conducting the investigation

Students should keep handling of the balloon to a minimum once it has been charged to avoid accidental discharge. They should gently bring the balloon close to the other balloon and observe what happens as it approaches and then meets the surface of the second balloon.

Students might charge one side of the balloon but bring the wrong side of the balloon towards the material. If this happens consistently, advise students to mark the side of the balloon that they are going to charge, to avoid confusion.

Supporting your students

Model the activity, based on the scenario of the balloon and wall. Select students to represent the particles in the balloon and the wall. Show the movement of the electrons backwards in the wall as the negatively charged balloon is brought towards it.

Challenging your students

Students could create a leaflet explaining how electrostatic induction occurs. They could direct this towards students in the year below, as an introductory guide. They should provide real-life examples, such as lightning strikes and the balloon against the wall, to convey how the phenomenon works.

Key discussion points for this investigation

- **Theory**: What is induced charge? How is it achieved? Why does the induced object become charged? Why do not all objects accept an induced charge?
- **Methodology**: How can a balloon be used to test the materials? How will an induced charge be measured? What variables will need to be controlled?
- **Results**: How will the results be presented? How can these results be manipulated to draw a conclusion?
- **Evaluation**: Does the prediction support the theory? How can reliable measurements be made? How effective was the method? Can any improvements be made?

Answers to workbook questions

1   Concrete, paper and pencil shavings can all be charged by induction. This was evidenced by the balloon becoming attracted towards the previously uncharged materials.
2   Once the balloon was charged it was handled only by means of the string or its tied end.
3   The time for which the balloon was charged, the material with which the balloon was charged, use the same balloon each time.

Answers to exam-style questions

1   By rubbing the rod against a woollen cloth, clothes, or by friction. [1]
2   Negative; [1] because opposite charges attract. [1]
3   Cotton. [1] It does not conduct electricity [1] / does not have free electrons / is an insulator. [1]
4   No. [1] Water conducts away the charge so the results would be less evident. [1]
5   The sphere would move away from the rod. [1]
                                                    Total marks [8]

18 Electrical quantities

Throughout this chapter your students will be expected to:
● manipulate apparatus to obtain observations or measurements
● take readings from an appropriate measuring device
● plan an experiment or investigation, including making reasoned predictions of expected results and suggesting suitable apparatus and techniques.

Practical investigation 18.1 Investigating current

Planning the investigation

During this investigation your students will:
● use and describe the use of an ammeter, both analogue and digital
● understand that the current at every point in a series circuit is the same
● state that, for a parallel circuit, the current from the source is larger than the current in each branch.

This investigation can be taught in conjunction with the theory. Some of the elements of this investigation will require pre-teaching about basic components. Students should be able to recognize, from work in previous years work, the basic symbols for the components used in this investigation but a quick refresher is advisable at the beginning of the session.

Duration: 30 minutes

Grouping: Ideally, students work in pairs, or a maximum of three to a group, so that they gain experience of setting up circuits from a diagram, but this will depend on availability of equipment and size of class.

Setting up for the investigation

Each group will need: 2 1.5 V cells, 2 bulbs, ammeter, connecting leads, push switch

A power pack can also be used but should be locked at 3 V if possible.

Distribute equipment evenly around the classroom edge to prevent clustering.

In part 1: students are asked to record the current, using an ammeter positioned in three different places in a circuit.

In part 2: they are asked to repeat the experiment for a parallel circuit. Based on their results students will be expected to draw a conclusion for current in series and parallel circuits.

Safety considerations

MH

Safety-check equipment before giving it to students. Remove any damaged wires from the set.

Common errors when conducting the investigation

Mainly, students have trouble setting up the circuits from a diagram. Check each group's circuit before they start the investigation to ensure they get the right answers. If this is their first time building a circuit, students might not be able to identify possible causes for why their circuit is not working. It is worth spending a few minutes at the beginning of the investigation, discussing reasons why circuits might not work.

Check the cell: show students how to do this.

Check that the ammeter works and is on the correct sensitivity setting before turning on the circuit.

Check the leads and check each lamp. Are they all connected correctly?

Suggest students work through these points if their circuit appears not to work. It will consume some time at the beginning of the session but will reduce the time spent checking problems later on. This is also a confidence builder for students.

Supporting your students

Students might need one-to-one support in setting up the equipment. A good way to familiarise them with the diagram is to get students to trace over it with their finger, setting up as they do, for example, finger on the cell, out of the positive terminal comes a wire (student sets up the wire out of the cell); follow the wire with your finger. It goes into an ammeter (student connects wire to ammeter) and so on, until the circuit is complete.

Challenging your students

Students could devise a practical to test potential difference in both series and parallel circuits. This should include circuit diagrams to support the work. Students should make predictions, based on their results from this investigation and their knowledge of the relation $V = IR$.

Key discussion points for this investigation

- **Circuits**: What are the common symbols for components? (lamp, wires, cell, ammeter) How are circuits set up from diagrams? What is a series circuit? Explain the difference between a series and parallel circuit.

- **Measurements**: How will students measure current? Units? What precision should they use? How is this represented in the table – all values should have the same degree of precision.
- **Conclusions**: How will students write a conclusion? What do the answers reveal? How can students incorporate the results into the conclusion?
- **Reliability**: Does it matter if results differ slightly? Why might this happen? Are the results reliable? (Yes – if there is only a small variation in the student's repeat results.) If someone else did this experiment would they achieve similar results? (No) How could students adapt this investigation to ensure that the results are reproducible?

Answers to workbook questions

1. The current in a series circuit is the same throughout the circuit.
2. The current in a parallel circuit is smaller down the branches than the current that is pushed out of the cell.
3. No. Current is not used up, it remains the same around a series circuit and the total current leaving and returning to the cell remains the same in a parallel circuit.
4. Ammeter. A digital ammeter gives a discrete reading but when using an analogue version, human error can occur in judging the point at which the needle lies.
5. The switch means that the circuit is off until turned on, which can reduce the heating effects of the current on the components.

Practical investigation 18.2
Determining the resistance

Planning the investigation

During this investigation your students will:

- describe an experiment to determine resistance using a voltmeter and an ammeter
- recall and use the equation $R = \frac{V}{I}$.

This investigation can be taught in conjunction with the theory.

Duration: 35 minutes

Grouping: Ideally, students work in pairs, or a maximum of three to a group, so that they gain experience of setting up circuits from a diagram, but this will depend on availability of equipment and size of class.

Setting up for the investigation

Each group will need: a variety of resistors, component holders, leads, 2 1.5 V cells, ammeter, voltmeter, push switch, heatproof mat

They will need at least four different resistors, for example, 33 Ω, 47 Ω, 56 Ω, 68 Ω, 100 Ω.

Distribute the equipment evenly around the outside edge of the classroom to prevent crowding. Students are asked to design an experiment to determine the resistance of different resistors. They have been provided with an equipment list and advised of safety precautions.

Safety considerations

MH

Circuits should be turned off when not in use to prevent burns from overheating.

A heatproof mat should be used to protect the surface from damage due to overheating.

Common errors when conducting the investigation

Mainly, students have trouble setting up the circuits correctly. They might place the ammeter and voltmeter in incorrect positions. Check all students' circuits before they proceed.

Supporting your students

Offer students help in setting up circuits, giving one-to-one help if necessary. A good way to familiarise them with the diagram is to get students to trace over it with a finger, setting up as they do, for example, finger on the cell, out of the positive terminal comes a wire (student sets up the wire out of the cell); follow the wire with a finger. It goes into an ammeter (student connects wire to ammeter) and so on, until the circuit is complete. Students might also struggle with the maths in this investigation. As a starter to the session, work through some basic $R = \frac{V}{I}$ examples and leave them on the board for reference.

Give students struggling with the method or circuit set-up a circuit diagram from which to work.

Challenging your students

Ask students to sketch a $V–I$ graph for each of the resistors in the experiment. Students should recognise that the gradient of the $V–I$ graph represents resistance, so the greater the resistance, the steeper the gradient. Students should then be asked to predict what the $I–V$ graphs for the resistors might look like.

Suggested discussion points for this investigation

- **Method**: How will students conduct their investigation? What measurements will they need to take? How will they measure voltage? How will they measure current?
- Do they know where to position a voltmeter in a circuit and why? Where should they position an ammeter in the circuit and why? Can they draw a circuit diagram of the set-up?
- **Safety**: Why should they use a push switch? Where should the heatproof mat be positioned and why?
- **Table of results**: What will be included in their table? How will they present the table? What must be included in the headings? How must the results be recorded (all to the same degree of precision).

Answers to workbook questions

1 The students complete a table for their results.

Resistor number	V/V			I/A		
1						
2						
3						
4						

2 The students calculate the resistances of their resistors.

3 Support: yes they are similar. All resistors have to meet industry standards so must have a resistance similar to its coding.
Against. No they differ significantly. This might be due to error in measuring devices, resistance between contacts in the circuit causing inaccurate measurments.

4 The ammeter should be placed in series within the circuit so it can measure the current in the circuit effectively.

5 Ammeter 0.01 A, voltmeter 0.01 V

6 Take up to three readings for each value of current and see if the results obtained are similar in value. If they are not, change the meters to see if there is an error in the equipment.

Practical investigation 18.3
Investigating current in components

Planning the investigation

During this investigation your students will:
- recall and use the equation $R = \dfrac{V}{I}$
- describe an experiment to determine resistance, using a voltmeter and an ammeter
- sketch and explain the current–voltage characteristic of an ohmic resistor and a filament lamp.

This investigation can be taught in conjunction with the theory.

Duration: 40 minutes

Grouping: Ideally, students should work individually so they can practise setting up circuits. However, if equipment is limited, students can work in groups of 2–4.

Setting up for the investigation

Each student or group will need: 100 Ω resistor, component holder, leads, heat-proof mat, ammeter, voltmeter, power supply,
The power supply should be locked off at 6 V if possible. Distribute the equipment evenly around the classroom to prevent crowding.
Students are asked to set up a given circuit, varying the p.d across a resistor, to take current readings. The students are then required to plot an I–V graph of the results and comment on what it represents.

Safety considerations

MH

Students should turn off power packs when they are not in use to prevent overheating in the resistor.
Make students aware that the power packs should not go above 6 V if they cannot be locked off.

Common errors when conducting the investigation

The main problem encountered by students is setting up a circuit from the diagram. Check each student's circuits before they start the investigation to ensure they get the right answers.
If this is their first time building a circuit, students might not be able to identify possible causes why their circuit is not working. It is worth spending a few

minutes at the beginning of the investigation, discussing reasons why circuits might not work.

Check the cell: show students how to do this.

Check that the ammeter works and is on the correct sensitivity setting before turning on the circuit.

Check the leads and check each lamp. Are they all connected correctly?

Suggest students work through these points if their circuit appears not to work. It will consume some time at the beginning of the session but will reduce the time spent checking problems later on. This is also a confidence builder for students.

Supporting your students

Students who struggle to set up circuits might need one-to-one help in how to set up. A good way to familiarise them with the diagram is to get students to trace over it with their finger, setting up as they do, for example, finger on the cell, out of the positive terminal comes a wire (student sets up the wire out of the cell); follow the wire with a finger. It goes into an ammeter (student connects wire to ammeter) and so on, until the circuit is complete.

Students might struggle to explain the relationship between current and voltage. Take students through this step by step, with a worked example. Display different graphical relationships on the board and discuss them as a class. This allows less able students to make the connection between the shapes of graph on the board and their results.

Challenging your students

Students could design an investigation to examine the current in other key components such as a diode, thermistor or filament lamp. They should also include an I–V graph for this investigation.

Key discussion points for this investigation

Theory: The heating effect of current can be demonstrated in this investigation and should also be discussed as a safety issue.

Graphs: What is an appropriate scale for the graph? How will students handle anomalous results? What is the implication of a straight-line graph? How is direct proportionality represented? What does the gradient represent?

Answers to workbook questions

1 The students record their results in their tables.

Potential difference, p.d./V	Current I/A

2 A graph of current against voltage should be drawn. A straight line graph through the origin with a gradient approximating to $100\,\Omega$

3 The current–voltage relationship is directly proportional. This means that, when the results are plotted, a straight-line graph through the origin is obtained.

4 The resistance of the student's resistor will be less. This is because the gradient represents $\frac{1}{R}$.

5 An ohmic conductor is a component that follows Ohm's law. This means the current is directly proportional to the potential difference across it.

6 Subtract the error from all values obtained.

7 Maintain the resistor's temperature when repeating readings.

Answers to exam-style questions

1. A, V, Ω all correct. [1]
2. 1 mark for each correct answer. [4]

V/V	I/A	R/Ω
2.00	0.080	25
1.40	0.034	41
2.00	0.024	83
1.20	0.012	100

3. Place the resistor on a heatproof mat to prevent damage to the surface; turn off the power pack when not in use to reduce effects of heating. [1]

4. Correct circuit symbols, [1] correct positioning of components, [1] straight lines for wires, drawn with a ruler. [1]

5. Suitable scale required, [1] axes labelled including units, [1] correct plot to $\frac{1}{2}$ square, [2] neatness of plot and line of best fit – are they all clear? [1]

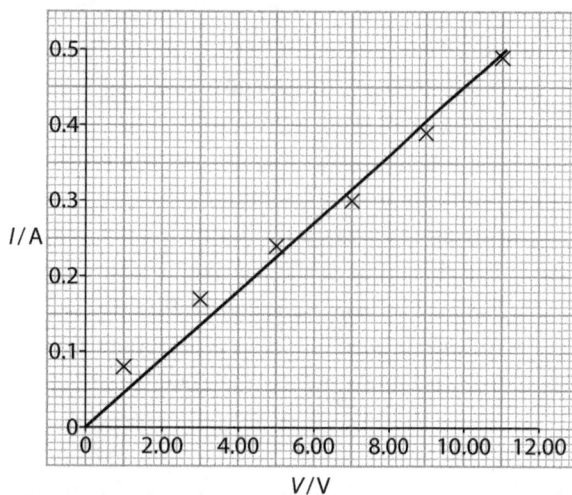

6. Triangulation method demonstrated, [1] 25, [1] Ω [1]

7. Yes, the student is correct.[1] It is a straight line graph that goes through the origin. [1]

Total marks [19]

19 Electric circuits

This chapter contains investigations on:

◆ **4.3.2** Series and parallel circuits

◆ **4.3.3** Action and use of circuit components

◆ **4.5** Dangers of electricity

Throughout this chapter your students will be expected to:
- draw, complete or label diagrams of apparatus
- draw an appropriate conclusion, justifying it by reference to the data and using an appropriate explanation
- make estimates or describe outcomes which demonstrate their familiarity with an experiment, procedure or technique.

Practical investigation 19.1 Light-dependent resistors

Planning the investigation

During this investigation your students will:
- describe the action of light-dependent resistors and show understanding of their use as input transducers
- describe the action of a diode and show understanding of its use as a rectifier
- recognise and show understanding of circuits operating as light-sensitive switches.

This investigation can be taught in conjunction with sensing circuits.

Duration: 45 minutes

Grouping: 2–4 per group dependent on equipment and class size. This can be conducted individually by those students who will be sitting a practical examination for experience of setting up circuits from instructions.

Setting up for the investigation

Each group will need: LDR, ohmmeter (or an ammeter in series to the LDR and a voltmeter in parallel to the LDR), 12 V lamp, power supply, black card

If no ohmmeter is available, use a voltmeter in parallel to the LDR and ammeter.

Black card is optional, students should recognise that this will make their results more reliable by filtering out the light from the surrounding room. It should be wrapped around the LDR to provide a discrete channel for the light.

If a lux meter is available, the investigation can be extended to measure the light intensity in lux, so that students can plot a graph of resistance against light intensity.

In this investigation, students will examine the relationship between light intensity and resistance. The depth to which this investigation is conducted depends on the availability of equipment. Students are asked to vary the distance from the light source (reducing the intensity of light) and use an ohmmeter to record the resistance. If lux meters are available they can measure the light intensity at different distances and plot a graph of the results.

Safety considerations

MH

Students should turn the circuit off when it is not in use, to prevent overheating of the lamp and reduce the risk of burns.

Common errors when conducting the investigation

Students might set up the circuit incorrectly, so check their circuits before allowing them to start. Those students whose circuits have been checked can act as 'student experts', checking the other groups' circuits against their own, whilst you check other groups. Students who are conducting an investigation into the effect of the distance from the light source might not recognise that as the distance increases then the light intensity decreases. When they are discussing their results and trying to formulate a conclusion, these students will need to recognise that as the distance increases the resistance also increases. The increase in distance represents a decrease in intensity.

To achieve reliable results, this experiment needs to be conducted in a dark room. Discuss this with the students at the beginning of the session, to get them thinking about reliability and the impact of the background light on their investigation. If it is not possible to darken the room by turning off the lights and drawing blinds, students can use tubes of card that have been painted black, to isolate the LDR.

Supporting your students

Students who find it difficult to set up circuits might need one-to-one support. A good way to familiarise them with the diagram is to get students to trace over it with their finger, setting up as they go, for example, finger on the cell, out of the positive terminal comes a wire (student sets up the wire out of the cell); follow the wire with their finger. It goes into an ammeter (student connects wire to ammeter) and so on, until the circuit is complete.

Some students might find it difficult to formulate a conclusion, due to the correlation between increasing distance and reducing light intensity. Offer support, either one-to-one or as a class.

Challenging your students

Students could research the effect of LDRs in common circuitry. For example, how would an LDR affect a street light, if it were fitted? In a camera if it controlled the shutter? Students should produce a poster, as if they were working for an LDR company, advertising the uses of the LDR to potential buyers.

Key discussion points for this investigation

- **Theory**: As the distance increases, what is the effect on the intensity of the light? How could this be measured more precisely? What equipment would be used to measure light intensity?
- **Conclusions**: How will students write a conclusion? What story do the answers tell? How can students incorporate the results into the conclusion?
- **Evaluation**: Does the prediction support the theory? How can measurements be made to be reliable? How effective was the method? Can any improvements be made?

Answers to workbook questions

1   The students record their results in the table, see exemplar results on CD-ROM.
2   The students plot a graph of resistance against distance.

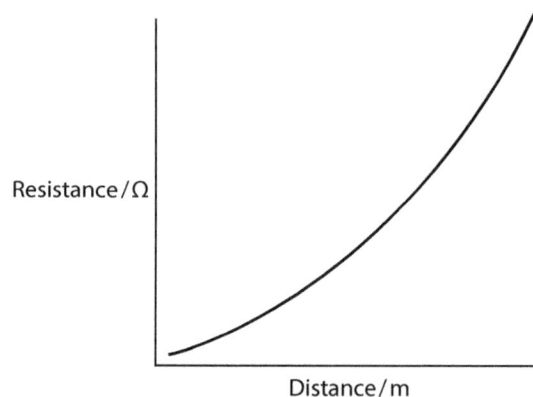

3   As the light intensity decreases the resistance increases; students should make reference to their results to support.
4   No. When the light intensity is low, the resistance is very high. This would stop the current from flowing around the circuit so the light would not turn on.
5   Placed the LDR inside a black tube of card that surrounded the light under investigation.
6   A light detector attached to a data logger could have been used at the set distances to measure the light intensity.

Practical investigation 19.2 Thermistors

Planning the investigation

During this investigation your students will:
- describe the action of thermistors and show understanding of their use as input transducers
- recognise and show understanding of circuits as temperature-operated alarms (to include the use of a relay).

This practical can be conducted in conjunction with the theory. This can be given as an extension task for more able students or run as a class practical over two lessons.

Duration: 60 minutes

Grouping: up to 4 per group

Setting up for the investigation

Each group will need: a thermistor, a beaker, hot water, a small plastic bag

The plastic bag is to protect the thermistor when it is immersed in the hot water.

If no ohmmeter is available, use a voltmeter in parallel to the thermistor. The ammeter should be placed in series to the thermistor.

Carry out the experiment before the session, to ensure the voltage and current are at safe levels for the thermistor being used.

In this practical, students are asked to design an investigation to determine the effect of temperature on the resistance of a thermistor. They are given a basic equipment list to which they can add. They will be expected to plot a graph of their results.

Safety considerations

MH

Students should conduct the investigation standing, to reduce the risk of scalding should the hot water be knocked over.

Students should cover the thermistor in the plastic bag and the connecting leads should also be protected with plastic.

Common errors when conducting the investigation

Remind students to start with hot water and record the temperature of the water, as it cools, and the corresponding resistance.

Supporting your students

Give students a circuit diagram from which to work. Students should immerse the thermistor in boiling water and have the thermistor connected to the ohmmeter. As the water cools, they should record the temperature of the water and the resistance of the thermistor and tabulate the results.

Challenging your students

Students could design and market a digital thermometer. They should produce a marketing flier that describes how the thermometer works, with an example of a circuit that might be present in the thermometer. Students should describe where the thermometer would be positioned to take its recording, what it will look like and who will be the target market.

Key discussion points for their investigation

- **Method**: How will students conduct their investigation? What measurements will they need to take? How will they measure the resistance? How will they draw a circuit diagram of the set up? Will they do a preliminary test? Why might this be beneficial?
- **Safety**: How will students protect themselves when using boiling water? How will they protect the circuit?
- **Table of results**: What will be included in the table of results? How will students present the table? What must be included in the headings? How must the results be recorded? (All to the same degree of precision.)
- **Graphs**: Discuss scaling, labels, units, curve of best fit. What relationship does the line of best fit illustrate?

Variables

Independent: temperature; dependent: resistance

Questions

1   The students tabulate their results, as shown in table below.

Temperature	Potential difference /V	Current /A	Resistance /Ω

2   The students plot a graph of resistance against temperature.

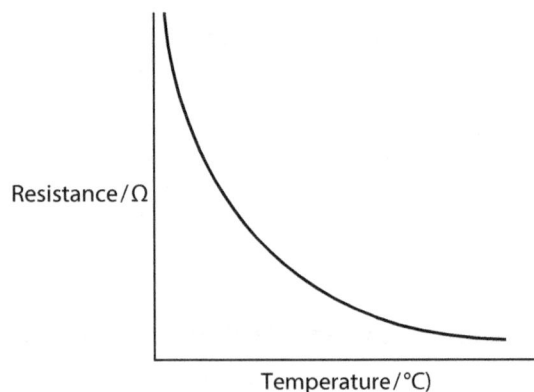

Resistance/Ω

Temperature/°C

3   For an NTC thermistor – as the temperature increases the resistance decreases. Students should refer to their own results, writing for example "This is illustrated in the experimental results. When the temperature is 40° the resistance is 250 Ω but drops to 100 Ω when the temperature increases to 70°."

4   Ensure readings on thermometer are taken from eye level; check for non-zero error on the ohmmeter before use; thermistor fully submersed in the water; water is stirred to ensure temperature reading is correct throughout the water. Read the thermometer at eye level to reduce parallax error; repeated readings and took an average to reduce error.

5   A voltmeter could be used in parallel to the thermistor and an ammeter in series in a circuit in order to calculate the resistance using the formula $R = \dfrac{V}{I}$.

Practical investigation 19.3
Investigating resistors in series and in parallel

Planning the investigation

During this investigation your students will:
- give the combined resistance of two or more resistors in series
- state that the combined resistance of two resistors in parallel is less than that of either resistor by itself
- recall and use the fact that the current from the source is the sum of the currents in the separate branches of a parallel circuit.

This investigation can be taught in conjunction with the theory.

Duration: 30 minutes

Grouping: 2–4 per group, dependent on equipment availability and class size. The activity can be conducted individually by those students who need experience of setting up circuits from circuit diagrams.

Setting up for the investigation

Each group will need: 3 10 Ω resistors, connecting leads, power supply at 6 V, ammeter, voltmeter, rheostat, switch

Three resistors of the same resistance are required. Distribute the equipment around the classroom to prevent clustering.

Students are asked to set up two circuits; one with three resistors in series and one with the same three resistors in parallel. They are asked to measure the potential difference and the current in the circuit, to ascertain the total resistance in the circuit. Students will then compare the total resistance in each circuit and draw a conclusion from this.

Safety considerations

MH

Circuits should be constructed on heatproof mats to prevent heat damage from resistors on the surface used. Students should turn off circuits when they are not in use to prevent overheating of the components.

Common errors when conducting the investigation

Students might connect the circuit incorrectly. Check the circuits before students start the investigation.

Supporting your students

Students might need help setting up the circuit. Students who find it difficult to set up circuits might need one-to-one support. A good way to familiarise them with the diagram is to get students to trace over it with their finger, setting up as they go, for example, finger on the cell, out of the positive terminal comes a wire (student sets up the wire out of the cell); follow the wire with their finger. It goes into an ammeter (student connects wire to ammeter) and so on, until the circuit is complete.

Challenging your students

Students could investigate other combinations of the resistors and record the total resistance in the circuit, to see how different ratios of resistances can be used to control the current in a circuit.

Key discussion points for this investigation

● **Theory**: Why does the effective resistance decrease in a parallel circuit? What is the relationship between the p.d. and the resistance in this instance?
● **Method**: How are the circuits set up? Where does the voltmeter go in each circuit? Why is it in this position? Why is the ammeter in series? How will students ensure it is in series in the parallel circuit? How have they ensured accuracy in this investigation? (Recording results for different values of V in each circuit.)

Answers to workbook questions

1 The students record their results in the tables.

2 The students draw circuit diagram for the second circuit.

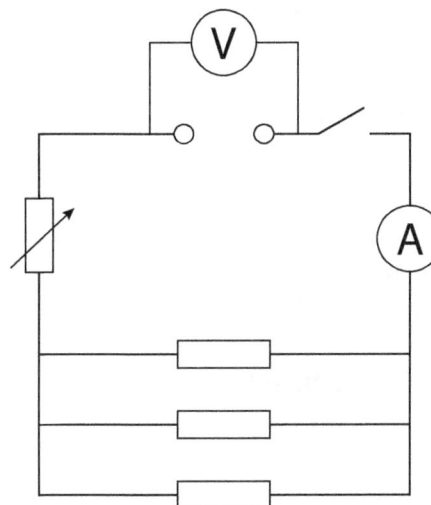

3 Students should calculate and record the resistance in both circuits using the formula $R = V/I$.

4 The total resistance in the parallel circuit is less than the resistance in the series circuit. Students should refer to their results to support. For example, this can be seen in the experimental results. The resistance in the parallel circuit is 3 Ω whereas in the series circuit it is 30 Ω.

5 A digital ammeter was used to prevent any errors in reading an analogue meter through parallax error.

Practical investigation 19.4 Investigating fuses

Planning the investigation

During this investigation your students will:

- state that a fuse protects a circuit
- explain the use of fuses and circuit breakers and choose appropriate fuse ratings and circuit-breaker settings.

This practical can be conducted in conjunction with teaching electrical safety.

Duration: 30 minutes

Grouping: 2–4 per group. This can be conducted individually by those students who need experience of setting up circuits from instructions.

Setting up for the investigation

Each group will need: 6 lamps, ammeter, 3 1.5 V cells, component holder, crocodile clips, leads, rheostat, cartridge fuse of 0.25 A

If 0.25 A cartridge fuses are not available, then a strand of wire wool can be used instead.

Distribute the equipment evenly around the classroom to prevent clustering.

Students are asked to set up a circuit of parallel lamps and record the total current flowing through it. They are then asked to set up a series circuit and increase the current until the fuse blows. Students record the current at this point.

Safety considerations

MH

Students should wear safety goggles to protect their eyes, should the fuse casing explode.

Common errors when conducting the investigation

Students might need help to construct the circuit from the circuit diagram. Check all circuits before students conduct the investigation.

Supporting your students

Students might need help setting up the circuit. Students who find it difficult to set up circuits might need one-to-one support. A good way to familiarise them with the diagram is to get students to trace over it with their finger, setting up as they go, for example, finger

on the cell, out of the positive terminal comes a wire (student sets up the wire out of the cell); follow the wire with a finger. It goes into an ammeter (student connects wire to ammeter) and so on, until the circuit is complete.

Challenging your students

Students could research the mechanism by which an RCD circuit-breaker works. They should construct an explanatory leaflet describing the process by which it operates.

Key discussion points for this investigation

- **Method**: How were lamps set up, both in series and in parallel?
- **Theory**: What does a fuse rating actually mean? The fuse can carry the current on the fuse rating for a short period of time but will break the fuse eventually. Why does it do this? If there were a surge in current how long would the fuse last?

Answers to workbook questions

1 The fuse did not blow because the current flowing through the circuit was lower than the rating value and so did not heat the fuse wire up enough to cause it to melt.

2 Yes. The fuse wire melted at a current similar to the rating on the fuse wire.

3 There is no parallax error so the result is more accurate. The digital ammeter reads to a greater number of decimal places so is more sensitive or precise.

4 The current in the circuit that causes the fuse to blow might be related to a p.d. that is between a whole-number interval. The rheostat allows for more sensitive readings to be taken.

Answers to exam-style questions

Voltmeter in parallel to all components or across the cell. [1]

1   See the table; all three = 2 marks; 2 = 1 mark; 1 = 0 [2]

Circuit	V/V	I/A	R/Ω	Appearance of the lamp
1	1.49	0.50	3.0	bright
2	1.48	0.22	4.5	dim

2   See the table, mark for each correct [2]

3   Circuit 1: bright; [1] circuit 2: dim [2]

4   If the student added another resistor in parallel to the other resistors in each of the circuits this would reduce the effective resistance of both circuits. Placing a resistor in parallel to another makes it easier for the current to flow reducing the total resistance in the circuit.

Total marks [9]

20 Electromagnetic forces

This chapter contains investigations on:

Throughout this chapter your students will be expected to:
- select the most appropriate apparatus or method for a task and justify the choice made
- make estimates or describe outcomes which demonstrate their familiarity with an experiment, procedure or technique.

Practical investigation 20.1 Making a relay circuit

Planning the investigation

During this investigation your students will:
- describe applications of the magnetic effect of current, including the action of a relay
- describe the effect on the magnetic field of changing the magnitude and direction of the current.

This practical can be conducted in conjunction with theory of electromagnetism.

Duration: 30 minutes

Grouping: ideally, students should work in pairs, depending on class size and availability of equipment.

Setting up for the investigation

Each group will need: copper wire, laminated C-core, (or a soft iron rod with enough coils around it to become magnetised when the 1.5V cell is connected), 1.5V cell, switch, any thin steel of nickel strip, clamp and two wooden blocks, 12 V power supply, 12 V lamp, tape

A hacksaw blade can be used as the steel strip but students must be cautious of the teeth on the blade. Set up the equipment in stations beforehand, to prevent the students from clustering. Students are asked to construct a basic relay circuit. The 1.5 V circuit will be used to turn on a 12 V lamp in a secondary circuit.

Safety considerations

MH

Ensure that the steel strips are demagnetised before use. If they are using hacksaw blades, students should handle them with care to reduce risk of cuts.

Common errors when conducting the investigation

The construction of the relay circuit can be difficult. Students should use the diagram as a reference to ensure they are constructing it correctly. Key technical points are:
- Ensure the steel strip is very close to the C-core but not touching it.
- If the 1.5 V circuit does not turn the 12 V circuit on, check that the contacts are touching at the end of the steel strip. Once the 1.5 V circuit is turned on the magnetic strip should be pulled downwards, causing the contacts to touch.
- If the magnet produced by the 1.5 V circuit is not strong enough, students should increase the number of turns on the C-core, up to a maximum of 50 turns.

Supporting your students

Demonstrate how to set up the circuit by displaying a prepared relay on the front bench. Less able students can use this as a reference point to check that their set-up is correct. They might require one-to-one support if they are really struggling, or they can use the displayed set-up if they are falling behind.

Challenging your students

Students could investigate real-life examples of relay circuits. They should put together an information leaflet explaining how relay circuits work and highlighting the safety benefits of a relay.

Suggested discussion points for this investigation

- **Theory**: Why is one circuit used to turn on another? What are the advantages/disadvantages of this? Discuss examples of where relay circuits are used, to illustrate the safety aspect, for example, in an electric shower switch, car ignition and some circuit breakers.
- **Method**: Why would a soft iron core be used in the primary circuit? Why is the core laminated? Why should the steel strip not touch the C-core when the circuit is turned off?

Answers to workbook questions

1. The lamp in the 12 V circuit is turned off.
2. The lamp in the 12 V circuit is turned on.
3. When the 1.5 V circuit is turned on, the C-core becomes magnetised and attracts the steel strip. As the steel strip moves downwards the contact wires touch, completing the 12 V circuit, causing the lamp to turn on.
4. This protects the user as the voltage in the 1.5 V circuit will be at a much safer level than in the 12 V circuit.
5. The blade must be made from steel, iron, cobalt or nickel as it needs to be attracted to the C-core to make a contact and complete the 12 V circuit.
6. Increase the current in the smaller circuit or increase the number of turns on the coil.

Practical investigation 20.2
The motor effect

Planning the investigation

During this investigation your students will:
- describe an experiment to show that a force acts on a current-carrying conductor in a magnetic field, mentioning the effect of reversing:
  - the current
  - the direction of the field.

This investigation can be taught in conjunction with the theory.

Duration: 30 minutes

Grouping: Ideally, students should work in pairs, or with a maximum of 4 per group, depending on availability of equipment and class size.

Setting up for the investigation

Each group will need: 4 circular disc magnets, tape, board, compass, a length of insulated copper wire, 2 1.5 V batteries connected with leads, crocodile clips
The circular disc magnets may be ceramic or ferrite.
The board should be 5 cm by 10 cm by 15 cm.
If possible, set up the equipment in tray packs before the session. If this is not possible, distribute the equipment evenly around the classroom to prevent crowding.
Students are asked to set up a magnetic field, using two pairs of circular magnets that have been arranged with a 1 cm channel between them. Students will place a current-carrying conductor inside the magnetic field between the magnets and observe the movement that takes place. Motor kits can be used to demonstrate the motor effect if available. All questions and discussion points will be applicable should a motor kit be used.

Safety considerations

The circuit should only be connected during observations, to prevent overheating.
Students must take care when handling the magnets so that they do not trap fingers when putting them together. Keep magnets away from mobile phones, bank cards and watches.

Common errors when conducting the investigation

Students will need to ensure the continuity of the

magnetic field across the 1 cm gap so they will need to ensure they have a south pole on one side and a north pole on the other.

Supporting your students

Students are likely to have trouble with the theory rather than the practical aspects. They should use **Fleming's left-hand rule for motors** to predict which way the wire will move. Allow students to write on their hands what each finger represents to support their use of the rule (first finger = field: second finger = current: thumb = motion).

Challenging your students

Students could produce an explanatory leaflet on the motor effect, explaining the left-hand motor rule. Students could create a fact file on Michael Faraday. It should include a summary of his ideas and findings on the motor effect and electromagnetic induction.

Key discussion points for this investigation

- **Theory**: Discuss Fleming's left-hand rule (LHR). How can students use this to predict the movement of the wire? Are the direction of the magnetic field and the direction of the current important? Use Fleming's LHR to predict where the wire will move before conducting the investigation.
- **Method**: How can they use a compass to find the direction of a magnetic field? Why is it important that the compass does not touch the magnet? How do they reverse the direction of the current down the wire?

Answers to workbook questions

1   The wire moved (and might be forced out of the magnetic field, depending on the polarity of their connection to the cell).
2   The wire moved in the opposite direction.
3   It will cause the wire to move in the opposite direction.
4   Fibreglass is an insulator and so will not conduct electricity, so the wire would not move.
5   Increase the current in the wire or increase the strength of the magnets.

Answers to exam-style questions

1   All three correct; [2] 2 correct [1]
2   As the circuit is turned on the rod will move [1] outwards [1]
3   The rod will move [1] in the opposite direction. [1]
4   Increase the current, [1] increase the power of the magnets. [1]
5   The copper rod is a conductor [1]

Total marks [9]

21 Electromagnetic induction

Throughout this chapter your students will be expected to:
- make estimates or describe outcomes which demonstrate their familiarity with an experiment, procedure or technique
- identify key variables and describe how, or explain why, certain variables should be controlled
- draw an appropriate conclusion, justifying it by reference to the data and using an appropriate explanation.

Practical investigation 21.1 Electromagnetic induction in a coil

Planning the investigation

During this investigation your students will:
- show understanding that a conductor moving across a magnetic field or a changing magnetic field linking with a conductor can induce an e.m.f. in the conductor
- describe an experiment to demonstrate electromagnetic induction
- state the factors affecting the magnitude of an induced e.m.f.

This investigation can be taught as an introduction to the theory of electromagnetic induction.

Duration: 20 minutes

Grouping: Ideally students should work in pairs, or a maximum of groups of 3.

Setting up for the investigation

Each group will need: insulated copper wire, cardboard tube, tape, galvanometer, bar magnet

The cardboard tube (optional) provides a base on which to coil the wire.

The galvanometer should have sensitivity between −3.5 mA and +3.5 mA.

Distribute the equipment around the classroom to prevent clustering. The students are asked to investigate what happens when:
- a magnet is pushed into a coil of wire
- the speed at which it is inserted is changed
- the number of coils on the wire is changed.

Safety considerations

Separate bar magnets with caution to avoid pinching of skin between magnets.

Common errors when conducting the investigation

Students might, without realising it, reverse the polarity of the magnet and so get conflicting results each time. Discuss the impact of the polarity of the magnet in the introductory part of the session, to avoid this.

If deflections on the galvanometer are too small, increase the starting number of turns on the coil. This investigation should be trialled before being conducted by students, to ascertain the correct base number of turns on the coil.

Supporting your students

It can be beneficial to have a station with the equipment set up, for demonstration purposes, on the front bench. This could be used for one-to-one support during the session or as a display for students to refer to, so they can see what the results should be.

Challenging your students

Students could use their results to sketch a graph of induced e.m.f. against time. This will allow them to correlate their results with the mathematical implications. Students could research how renewable energy sources such as wind turbines; hydroelectric dams and geothermal power stations produce electricity. They should include a description of the similarities and differences to generation in a power station.

Key discussion points for this investigation

- **Theory**: Electromotive force (e.m.f.) is induced in the wire. A galvanometer measures small currents. Students should be made aware that it is possible to have an induced e.m.f. and no current present. Why are there positive and negative values for current? Discuss Fleming's right-hand rule.
- **Equipment**: Why use a galvanometer rather than an ammeter? A galvanometer has a greater sensitivity so can detect smaller currents. Ammeters may be used for more powerful generators.
- **Conclusion**: How will students include their observations in their conclusion? Can conclusions lead on to further investigation? How could they adapt this investigation to obtain data to support their conclusions?

Answers to workbook questions

1 When the magnet is pushed inside the coil of wire the arm on the galvanometer deflects. Students should provide a reading.
2 When removing the magnet the arm of the galvanometer will deflect in the opposite direction. Students should provide a reading.
3 When the magnet remains in the coil the arm of the galvanometer should not deflect.
4 The arm of the galvanometer deflects further each way.
5 The arm of the galvanometer deflects further and faster each way.
6 The greater the number of turns, the greater the induced e.m.f. so the greater the current induced.
7 The faster the movement of the magnet within the coil, the greater the induced e.m.f. and thus the greater the induced current.
8 Dependent variable: induced e.m.f. or current; independent variable: number of coils
9 The size of the magnetic field; keep the magnets the same throughout. The speed at which the magnet is inserted into the coil; insert into the coil at a consistent speed.
10 It has a greater sensitivity than an ammeter so will detect smaller currents and can also indicate the direction of current flow.

Practical investigation 21.2 Investigating transformers

Planning the investigation

During this investigation your students will:
- describe the construction of a basic transformer with a soft-iron core, as used for voltage transformations
- recall and use the equation $\frac{V_p}{V_s} = \frac{N_p}{N_s}$
- understand the terms 'step-up' and 'step-down'
- describe the principle of operation of a transformer.

Duration: 20 minutes.

Grouping: This is a teacher-led investigation.

Setting up for the investigation

You will need: transformer with detachable iron yoke, 4 m insulated copper wire, 1200-turn primary coil, 2.5 V bulb with holder

The insulated copper wire should be approximately 4 m in length to enable you to increase the number of turns Turn the transformer off when it is not in operation to reduce the heating effect in the primary coil.

Position and set up the equipment in good view of the class. Demonstration method

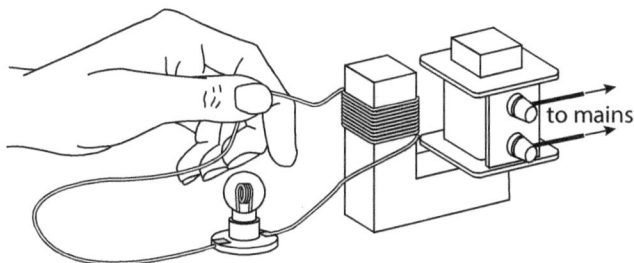

Figure 21.1

Set up the transformer so that the 1200-turn primary coil is mounted and connected to the mains supply (see Fig. 21.1). **Do not turn on** at this point. Discuss with students the key features of the transformer, for example, the laminated iron core, the primary and secondary coils. Discuss the importance of the a.c. supply and the changing magnetic flux and why it will only work in this configuration. Ask students why a DC will not work. Wrap 20 turns on the secondary coil and connect it to the bulb. Turn on the mains. Reiterate the process to the students, discussing how it is possible to see light in the bulb.

Increase the number of turns on the secondary coil. Ask: *What happens to the brightness of the bulb? How does it do this? What is the p.d. across the primary coil? How is the transformer behaving?* Suggest the ideas of step-up and step-down transformers. Add on the iron yoke.

Ask: *Why does the bulb increase in brightness? What impact is the yoke having on the magnetic flux?*

Safety considerations

MH

To reduce the risk of over-heating, turn the transformer off when it is not in use. The primary coil will heat up rapidly if left connected to the mains.

Common errors when conducting the investigation

Trial the demonstration before performing it in front of the group, to ensure that 20-turn increments show enough of a difference in brightness of the bulb.

Supporting your students

Students will struggle to understand how the transformer induces a p.d. in the second coil. They often confuse the magnetic flux with the current and believe it is flowing through the iron core to the secondary coil. Give a step-by-step guide to how the transformer works so the students can see the process broken into small segments.

Challenging your students

These students could use the ratios to predict the brightness of the lamp.

They should research the use of transformers in the national grid and describe the role of the step-up and step-down transformers in the safe delivery of electricity to homes.

Answers to workbook questions

1 The lamp is dimly lit when there are 20 turns on the primary coil.

2 Students should make a prediction and give reasoning to support their prediction.

3 The brightness of the lamp increases as the number of turns increases.

4 Students state whether their observation supports their prediction.

5 Prediction related to an increase in brightness. Reason: adding the yoke increases the magnetic flux in the transformer and so will increase the induced e.m.f. in the secondary coil.

6 State with reason if their observation supports their prediction.

7 A step down transformer. The mains voltage is 230 V but the bulb has a p.d. of 2.5 V so the voltage across the secondary is lower than that across the primary.

8 No. The alternating p.d. in the primary coil causes an alternating magnetic field in the soft iron core. This alternating magnetic field then induces an alternating p.d in the secondary coil.

9 A voltmeter could be connect in parallel to the AC supply on the primary and the lamp on the secondary coil.

Answers to exam-style questions

1 Independent variable: speed of rotation; dependent variable: the induced e.m.f.; control variable: the magnetic field strength; number of turns on the coil [3]

2 Keep the magnets the same each time. Maintain a constant number of coils of wire. [1]

3 A voltmeter [1]

Total marks [5]

22 The nuclear atom

This chapter contains investigations on:

◆ **5.1.1** Atomic model

◆ **5.1.2** Nucleus

Throughout this chapter your students will be expected to:
- make estimates or describe outcomes that demonstrate their familiarity with an experiment, procedure or technique
- draw an appropriate conclusion, justifying it by reference to the data and using an appropriate explanation.

Practical investigation 22.1
The structure of the atom

Planning the investigation

During this investigation your students will:
- describe the structure of an atom in terms of a positive nucleus and negative electrons
- describe the composition of the nucleus in terms of protons and neutrons
- use the term nuclide and use the nuclide notation
- use and explain the term 'isotope'.

This practical can be taught in conjunction with the theory.

Duration: 20 minutes

Grouping: Students work in pairs.

Setting up for the investigation

Each group will need 30 beads (3 sets of 10 each set in a different colour), a paper plate and string (optional). Provide sets of three different beads or counters with pots labelled, protons, neutrons and electrons. Each different colour should represent a different subatomic particle. The smallest of the beads/counters should represent the electrons.

The paper plate – or any circular disc – represents the atom.

Coloured string could be used to represent the orbitals. Distribute the equipment around the sides of the classrooms so that students do not cluster. Ask students to construct atoms of $^{14}_{7}$N, $^{12}_{6}$C, $^{4}_{2}$He and $^{7}_{3}$Li. They will use the beads or counters as models for protons, neutrons and electrons.

They will then adapt the atoms they have made into isotopes of the elements listed above.

Safety considerations

Beads could cause a slipping hazard, so students should keep them in small pots on the bench.

Remind students not to place the beads in their mouths as they pose a choking risk.

Common errors when conducting the investigation

Students are often confused about what changes in an isotope. Remind them that the number of neutrons changes, the numbers of protons and electrons remain the same. Discuss this as a class at the beginning of the session.

Supporting your students

Display a periodic table and encourage students to refer to it. This will enable them to recognise that the **nucleon number** defines the element. Students will soon identify that if the number of protons changes then they are changing the **element** rather than creating an isotope.

Challenging your students

Students could investigate what happens in fission and fusion and devise a way to model this to the class. They should prepare a 2-minute presentation for the class.

Key discussion points for this investigation

- **Model**: What are the components of the model representing? Encourage students to deduce this on their own; if necessary, guide them to the correct answer (plate – atom; beads or counters – protons, neutrons, and electrons; string – orbitals).
- **How has the idea of the atom evolved over time**? How can the model be adapted to show a more accurate representation? Discussion of the Bohr model and how it has evolved into the model of the atom we now accept.
  Similarities/differences:
  Similarities: there are three different types of particle/bead.; they are arranged similarly. Differences: There is no empty space in this model. The sizes of the atom and particles and spacing are not proportionate/representative of those in the atom
- **Theory**: Where are the particles positioned? How do we know this? Why are isotopes different within elements? Why do the elements not change if the nuclei are different?

Answers to workbook questions

1   Each different type of bead represents a different sub-atomic particle. The proton and neutron beads are collected in the centre of the plate in the nucleus, while the electron beads are positioned as orbitals on the outer edges of the plate.

2   **Similarities**: There are three different types of particle (bead); they are arranged similarly. **Differences**: There is no free space in this model. The sizes of the atom and particles and spacing are not proportionate or representative of those in the atom.

3   Include orbitals for electrons, make the model three-dimensional, create free space in the model.

4   There is free space between the planets; the planets orbit a central core (sun/nucleus), and the distances are more proportionate than the bead model.

Practical investigation 22.2
The alpha scattering experiment

Planning the investigation

During this investigation your students will:
- describe the structure of an atom in terms of a positive nucleus and negative electrons
- describe how the scattering of α-particles by thin metal foils provides evidence for the nuclear atom.

This practical can be conducted in conjunction with the theory.

Duration: 30 minutes

Grouping: class demonstration or in groups

Setting up for the investigation

You will need for demonstration: Nine 2-litre plastic bottles filled with sand or water for stability, table tennis balls weighted (injected with water) or another type of ball similar in size. A ramp can be made easily from a curved piece of plastic rail fixed to a wooden block, but this is optional. This can also be done on a smaller scale using 1 litre plastic bottles and marbles/large steel ball bearings. It is also possible to do this demonstration using a pre bought analogue kit.

Organise the equipment so that it is visible to all members of the class. The students are asked to make observations on how the model represents alpha particles being fired at gold foil.

Safety considerations

Precautions should be taken to ensure the table tennis balls do not bounce. Balls could be injected with water to weight them or ensure rolling on a smooth surface.

Common errors when conducting the investigation

If the surface is not smooth, unweighted table tennis balls will kick up and continue to bounce spoiling the demonstration. The speed the balls are fired at needs to be as constant as possible to show comparative deflections. If using a ramp, mark the release point for continuity.

Supporting your students

Students may have difficulty in seeing the deflection, so use talcum powder sprinkled lightly on the floor to show the deflection clearly. Some students may find linking the analogy difficult. This will take clear explanation. Students may benefit from pictures or a handout with the key parts of the analogy documented. For example:

The bottle represents the contents of an atom in gold foil. The table tennis balls represent the alpha particles being fired at the gold foil.

The nuclear force is represented by the curvature of the bottle so this will need to be discussed.

Challenging your students

Suggest that the students design another model for the alpha scattering experiment. They should devise their model, explaining what each element of the model represents and how they can demonstrate the angles of deflection of the alpha scattering.

Key discussion and demonstration points

- **Model**: What do the components of the model represent? Encourage students to deduce this on their own; if necessary, guide them to the correct answer. The bottle represents the contents of an atom. The nuclear force is not clearly represented in this model but reference can be made to the curvature of the bottle indicating the strength of the nuclear force. Methods of improving representation of the nuclear force can be discussed.
- **Differences in the model**: Discuss the difference between this simulation and the actual results of Rutherford's scattering model. Use the data on the CD-ROM to illustrate how only very small numbers of particles showed a large deflection. Most of the particles passed through the atom with little or no deflection at all, which indicated the vast space within the atom.
- **Similarities in the model**: the alpha particles are much smaller than the nucleus so the nucleus would not deflect on a collision but the alpha particle will in order to conserve momentum. The large spacing between the nuclei of the atom allows for many of the table tennis balls to pass through without

collision. If the balls hit the outer edge of the bottle they will deflect rather than rebound.

- **What are the differences?** The model does not represent the proportion of alpha particles that had minimal deflection in comparison to those that were reflected straight back. The model represents one gold atom but does not show the interaction between the alpha particles and numerous gold atoms. The relative proportions of the components of the model are not accurate, they do not represent the ratio of the sizes of the particles and the atom, nor of the spaces between the atoms. Proportion of size is not correct. There is limited free space in this model. This model shows one alpha particle to one target atom – Rutherford's experiment involved thousands of alpha nuclei to millions of atoms.
- **Adapting the model to show a more accurate representation**: Use more bottles, evenly spaced. If they are arranged close together, the table tennis balls will deflect. This is not true to Rutherford's results. How could students adapt this to allow some to pass straight through? (Move the bottles further apart.)
- **Demonstration**: Select a speed at which to roll the balls. This represents the energy with which the alpha particles are fired. Fire the balls towards the bottle arrangement from different positions to show that the majority will pass through, some will deflect slightly and the odd one or two will completely rebound. Discuss why these deflections might have been rare in Rutherford's results? Why might they have occurred? What does this imply about the nucleus? (Positive in charge; extremely small in comparison to atom size.)
- Fire subsequent balls in a line parallel to the centre of one bottle. This should cause a lesser deflection each time the trajectory of the balls is moved further out from the centre of the bottle. Why does the deflection lessen, the further the alpha particle is from the centre? How will increasing the speed of the particle impact upon the deflection? How can this be demonstrated in this model? (Increase the speed at which the ball is released.)

Answers to workbook questions

1) The balls represent the alpha particles. The bottle represents the contents of an atom and the curvature of the bottle represents the nuclear force of the atom.

2) The ball moves collides with the bottle and rolls back in the same direction.

3) The ball deflects away from the bottle as it collides with the side of the bottle.

4) The more off-axis the impact, the smaller the deflection of the table tennis ball from the centre of the bottle.

5) The ball deflects fully because the curvature is at its greatest at this point.

6) The size of the nucleus is small in comparison to the size of the atom so the alpha particles would rarely come head on to the nucleus.

7) Both models of the atom include positive and negative charges. The negative charge is significantly smaller in size compared to the positive charge. Other valid examples can also be excepted.

8) Rutherford's model: contains a positive central charge, the majority of the atom is free space. JJ Thomspon's model: positive "pudding" that fills the entirety of the atom, small negative charges contained throughout the atom

9) Similarities in the model: a large number of balls would pass through the model, balls will deflect with a greater angle the closer to the centre of the bottle they are fired.

10) Model represents one gold atom but does not show the interaction between the alpha particles and numerous gold atoms. The scale of the components in the demonstration does not reflect the proportions of the items they are representing. There is limited free space in this model.

Answers to exam-style questions

1   Electrons; [1] negative charge. [1]
2   Alpha particles fired at a thin gold foil; [1] the angles through which the alpha particles are scattered were measured; [1] a large number passed through but only a few deflected [1] showed the atom was made up of free space and a positive centre. [1]
3   They do not have a charge. [1]

Total marks [7]

23 Radioactivity

Throughout this chapter your students will be expected to:
- describe precautions taken in carrying out a procedure to ensure safety
- present and analyse data graphically, including the use of best-fit lines where appropriate, interpolation and extrapolation, and the determination of a gradient, intercept or intersection
- draw an appropriate conclusion, justifying it by reference to the data and using an appropriate explanation.

Practical investigation 23.1 Radioactive decay model

Planning the investigation

During this investigation your students will:
- use the term half-life in simple calculations, which might involve information in tables or decay curves
- calculate half-life from data or decay curves from which background radiation has not been subtracted.

This can be taught in conjunction with the theory.

Duration: 30 minutes

Grouping: 2–3 students per group. Depending on time and equipment availability, this can also be done as a whole-class exercise. Students all roll their dice at the same time and the data is collated on the board. Doing it this way can be quite chaotic and is often more time-consuming, but will give a smoother curve.

Setting up for the investigation

Each group will need: 25 dice, a tray

The dice can be replaced by wooden cubes, each with one face painted black, which can be purchased or made. Coins or counters can also be used.

Students are asked to roll the cubes, each time removing any that land on a 6/black side up. They will then plot a graph of their results, which will mimic a decay curve.

Safety considerations

There are no safety considerations for this investigation.

Common errors when conducting the investigation

Remind students to remove the dice that land with the 6-side facing upwards. Otherwise, the results will not mimic a decay curve.

Supporting your students

Students often have difficulty with the definition of half-life. They might not understand how to use the graph to find the half-life and the amount of undecayed atoms.

Challenging your students

Students could research how the half-life of uranium can be used to date the universe. They should devise a 2-minute presentation and include why uranium is used for this dating and how has it been used to date the universe.

Students could investigate the effects of radioisotopes on the body. They should produce an A4 poster documenting both the dangers of radioisotopes and the purpose and benefits of using them in medicine.

Key discussion points for this investigation

- **Model**: Discuss the theory behind the model before starting the investigation, so that students are clear about what the model represents. Initially the dice represent undecayed nuclei in a radioactive sample. When a die is thrown and it turns up a number six/ black face, this represents a decayed nucleus. The model should show that whilst it is not possible to pinpoint which nulcei will decay (each die will turn up a 6 or black face), over a period of time (a number of rolls) a pattern of decay will emerge. The time it takes for half of the nuclei to decay in a sample is known as the sample's half-life and this is different for each radioisotope.

- **Safety/theory**: Why might it not be safe or possible for students to conduct this, using radioactive sources? Discuss safety considerations for handling radioactive sources. Would increasing the sample size affect the half-life? If not, why not? Why are models useful to explain theory?

- **Graphs**: Why is the graph a curve? What relationship does this imply? How can the half-life be determined graphically? Given the half-life, how can the amount of undecayed atoms be determined graphically?

Answers to workbook questions

1   Students should record their results in the table. Results should range from 25 die remaining to 1 die remaining.
2   The students draw a graph of a decay curve, based on their results.

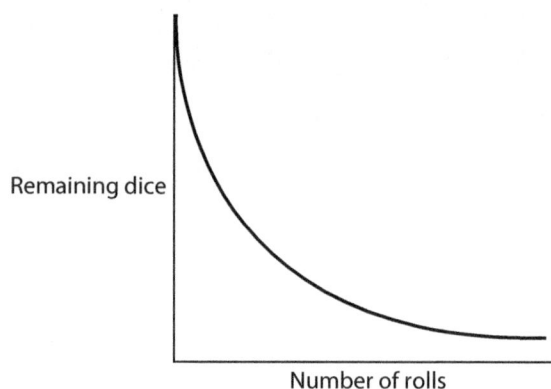

3   The students draw the curve of best fit on the graph.
4   Half-life is 4 throws, based on model data.
5   The half-life results are similar. This is representative of radio-isotopes of the same element. Each time the dice are thrown there is the same probability that a die will turn up a 6/ black face. This will give rise to the same decay pattern.
6   15 dice, based on the model data.
7   If the sample size is increased to 50 the half-life will remain the same.

Answers to exam-style questions

1   $164 \div 3$ [1] $= 55$ (2 sf) [1]

2   Any 2 from: artificial sources; cosmic rays; food and drink; radon; ground and buildings; medical [2]

3   Any 2 from: sources should be kept in a lead lined box in a metal storage box; should bear the radioactive symbol on the box; should be handled with tongs; students should stand a safe distance from the source; do not direct the source at anyone. [2]

4   As the thickness of the aluminium sheet increases, the amount of beta-decay passing through decreases, [1] supporting reference from data. [1]

5   Any 1 from; use same detector, same distance of source from the sheet. [1]

6   Repeat the investigation and take an average of the results. [1]

Total marks [10]